CREATION, FALL & THE HOPE OF REDEMPTION

a Commentary on Genesis 1 - 11

Bill Randles

CREATION, FALL & THE HOPE OF REDEMPTION:
A Commentary on Genesis 1 - 11

Copyright © 2016 Bill Randles

Published by:
Believers in Grace Ministries
8585 C Avenue
Marion, Iowa 52302

ISBN: 9780692715123

For more information about the author or his ministry, contact Billlrandles.Wordpress.com or believersingrace.com.

Except where otherwise indicated, all Scripture quotations in this book are taken from the King James Version of the Bible.

PRINTED IN THE UNITED STATES OF AMERICA

Contents

Genesis 1-11
Foundations for Faith

In the Lord put I my trust: how say ye to my soul, Flee as a bird to your mountain? For, lo, the wicked bend their bow, they make ready their arrow upon the string, that they may privily shoot at the upright in heart. **If the foundations be destroyed, what can the righteous do?** *The Lord is in his holy temple, the Lord's throne is in heaven: his eyes behold, his eyelids try, the children of men. The Lord trieth the righteous: but the wicked and him that loveth violence his soul hateth. Upon the wicked he shall rain snares, fire and brimstone, and an horrible tempest: this shall be the portion of their cup. For the righteous Lord loveth righteousness; his countenance doth behold the upright (Psalm 11).*

THE FIRST ELEVEN CHAPTERS of the Book of Genesis amount to the foundation of faith. In this divine revelation given to us through Moses, we are given the *how, why,* and the *what for,* of everything foundational to humanity.

It is the divine account of the origin of the universe and

all of life, of the creation and value of man and woman, the foundation of marriage, the roles of male and female, and of the value of children.

God tells us what went wrong with the world and with man, in the account of the Fall. The section also reveals something of man's deepest adversary, and the timeless methods of deception and seduction, which he uses to lead men astray from God. The deep questions of evil, suffering and death are explained in the first eleven chapters of Genesis.

Not only is the Fall of man explained, but the way of salvation is also partially revealed in these earliest chapters of Scripture. The primal gospel is the promise of the *"seed of the woman"*, who would one day come to *"crush the serpent's head"*, but not without excruciating pain, for the serpent, we are told, would *"bruise the heel"* of the woman's seed, in the process.

Other doctrines contained in this revelation include the worldwide flood, the ark of Noah, the way the world changed from the *"world that was"*, as Peter called it, to the "world that now is . . .", the incredible family tree in Genesis 10, the so-called "Table of the Nations", and finally the story which has universal and timeless application, that of the Tower of Babel.

It is my position that Genesis is a revelation of God. It is His explanation of that which is foundational to man, and to our understanding of the condition of man and the earth.

I believe that even the structure of the book is an act of God--laid out in the order of God's priorities.

God wanted us first to understand His Creation in six days and the meaning of Sabbath rest, (chapter 1). He then wanted to telescope the narrative, to cause us to take a closer look at the care He took in creating man and woman, and the ordination of marriage, (chapter 2).

Next, He wanted us to see what went wrong with the world, how we were deceived by the serpent and put into this terrible condemnation, and why there is suffering, vanity and death in this current age. But He also wanted us to see that in the midst of the calamity that is the Fall, there is the promise of salvation and restoration, (chapter 3).

Furthermore, God wanted there to be a sample contrast between two of Adam's sons, to show us the development of the only "two ways" that all men would follow. In Genesis 4, God shows the development of the God-rejecting line of Cain. God would have us see that, though fallen, man yet has dominion over creation, as expressed in Cain's line, through the development of metallurgy, animal husbandry, and the arts. This, though, doesn't perfect him or undo the sentence of spiritual and eventually physical death.

I find it interesting, that another early priority of God is to show us how it is that cities came into being, (Genesis 4).

Remember, these are the divine priorities, as to what constitutes the fundamental knowledge of the human condition and the way of salvation.

Genesis 5 walks us through the graveyard. We are called upon to contemplate the "wages of sin . . ." by the chronology of the line of Adam through Seth. People are born, they beget and then they die. But you will see that there is an amazing prophecy hidden in the meaning of the names of these faithful ones.

The worldwide flood, and the events leading up to it, as well as the changes which followed it, are another absolute "must know", according to the Creator. A person cannot ever hope to understand what is really happening in this world, without having taken these points from Genesis 1-11 into serious consideration.

Jesus said that the story of the Flood has eschatological inferences. *"As in the days of Noah, so shall the coming of the Son of Man be . . ."* Thus, the beginning is found again at the end. Peter tells us that one must be "willfully ignorant" to not see the effects of the Flood in this world.

Finally, the priority of the Creator and Judge of all the earth is that the one who is truly instructed would understand the meaning of the Tower of Babel incident. We cannot begin to understand our world, nor modern human affairs without the story of the world's first universal apostasy, and the divine judgment which dashed it to futility.

One cannot hope to begin to understand God, the world, humanity, salvation, evil, suffering, the past, present or future, without a true acceptance of the revelation given us in Genesis 1-11. It is truly the foundation for faith.

I make no attempt to justify my belief in the literality of Genesis 1-11. The Lord Jesus believed in all of it, as did Peter, James, John and the apostles, incorporating the stories of Adam, Eve, the Flood, and the serpent, into their teachings without qualification.

To Jesus, the Fall was a real event, with real consequences. He referred to the serpent as a *"murderer from the beginning . . ."* in John 8, and in an argument with the Pharisees about marriage, Jesus quoted Genesis 1 and 2 to make His point.

Jesus cited Abel as the first of the martyred prophets in Matthew 23:35, and warned that the time of His coming, would be *"as in the days of Noah"* in Matthew 24:37. John Whitcomb makes the point that one cannot discard Genesis 1-11 and at the same time consider Jesus a reliable guide to truth.

> It is the privilege of these men to dispense with an historical Adam if they so desire. But they do not at the same time have the privilege of claiming that Jesus Christ spoke the truth. Adam and Jesus Christ stand or fall together, for Jesus said: "If ye believed Moses, ye would believe me. But if ye believe not his writings, how shall ye believe my words?" (John 5:46-47). Our Lord also insisted

that "till heaven and earth pass away, one jot or one tittle shall in no wise pass from the law (and this includes Genesis) till all things be accomplished" (Matthew 5:18). If Genesis is not historically dependable, then Jesus is not a dependable guide to all truth, and we are without a Savior. [1]

The New Testament cites Genesis 200 times—more than half of them being citations from Genesis 1-11, (63 of those references referring to the first three chapters of Genesis).

Consider the Apostles Peter and Paul. Peter bases his teachings on baptism on the Flood, (1 Peter 3:18), even referring to *the angels which sinned in the days of Noah".* In 2 Peter, the physical evidence of the Flood becomes a witness to an unbelieving world of the final cataclysmic judgment to come.

Paul spoke of Eve being seduced by the serpent (2 Corinthians 11), and Adam being the original man (Romans 5). In his teaching on salvation, Paul contrasted Adam's one act of disobedience with the one act of the obedience of Christ, as the divine reasoning behind our salvation!

> For as by one man's disobedience many were made sinners, so by the obedience of one shall many be made righteous (Romans 5:19).

No wonder the author Ed Wharton warned us about the danger to our very concept of salvation, when scholars try to "mythologize" Genesis.

> A rejection of the biblical record of man's fall and of God's redemptive acts as historically factual has severe implications relative to the necessity and reliability of redemptive Christianity. When the Old Testament is not viewed as reliable history, the New Testament naturally comes under suspicion. For if the Genesis account of man's fall is not

accepted as a reality, what can make redemption through Christ a necessity? If mankind did not actually fall through sin, from what would he need saving? The Old Testament presents the origin of man, his fall, and his inability to redeem himself and so educates him to his need for salvation. The New Testament presents Christ as the satis- faction of that need. Thus both testaments form a unity of narrative and of purpose. Their accounts are so interrelated that they cannot be separated and at the same time maintain that redemption is a human necessity . . . If therefore Genesis is not literally true, then Jesus as presented in the gospels is simply not necessary. [2]

On the contrary, the Bible Scholar E. J. Young says of Genesis 11:

Genesis one is not poetry or saga or myth, but straightforward, trustworthy history, and, inasmuch as it is a divine revelation, accurately records those matters of which it speaks. That Genesis one is historical may be seen from these considerations: (1) It sustains an intimate relationship with the remainder of the book. The remainder of the book (i.e., The Generations) presupposes the Creation Account, and the Creation Account prepares for what follows. The two portions of Genesis are integral parts of the book and complement one an- other. (2) The characteristics of Hebrew poetry are lacking. There are poetic accounts of the creation and these form a striking contrast to Genesis one.[3]

Finally, I would like to explain my method in this commentary. I am not trying to be an academic; I am no Hebrew or Greek scholar, though I use the scholarship of respected Evangelical theologians with gratitude.

I am simply seeking to teach the meaning of the text, to put it on a level a layman can appreciate, as well as to tie into the text, other related Scripture. I am eager to demonstrate the fact that there is an unbroken continuity between the two "Testaments". The themes of Genesis 1-11 are developed throughout the rest of Scripture, coming to a complete expression at the end of Scripture and of time.

The ultimate hope of this author is that the reader will be led into a personal saving knowledge of the Lord and Savior revealed in Scripture. All of these teachings have a personal application.

For example: consider the doctrine of the fall of man. Genesis 3 is not merely a historical and academic account. Each one of us has a participation in the fall of man; because of it, we personally have been estranged from God, and are currently under a condemnation. We, too, need the intervention of the "seed of the woman" to free us from bondage to the serpent!

I PRAY FOR MY readers that this little volume will edify, exhort and strengthen you, bringing you into the saving and personal knowledge of God our Father and the Lord Jesus Christ.

1

Creation

In the beginning God created the heaven and the earth. (Genesis 1:1)

THE OPENING VERSE OF the Book of Genesis is a terse summation of reality.

- There was a beginning to all things.
- God was there.
- It was He who created everything that exists.
- What He created consists of time, space and matter.
- God the Creator is distinct from His creation.

Genesis 1:1 is indeed a theological statement, but it has also undergirded our Western concepts of science, technology, philosophy, and epistemology (the concept of truth).

Thus, the departure from Genesis 1:1 and all that follows it, has been the deepest and perhaps least appreciated reason for our current cultural decline and collapse. We have literally abandoned our foundations.

The *beginning* speaks of time. The *heavens* speak of space, and the *earth* speaks of matter. God created time, space and matter.

Genesis 1 refers exclusively to God as *Elohim*, a name that emphasizes the limitless power of the Deity. *Elohim* is a plural word suggesting that God is a unity yet in some sense a plurality. The Creator uses the plural expression, of and to Himself *"Let us make man in our image . . ."* on the sixth day of Creation. Thus the mystery of God's being is intimated from the beginning of the Bible.

God is distinct and separate from His creation. The creation is an expression of God, but it is not God, nor is it part of God. God is Holy. This means that God is entirely "other" than His creation. He is separate and "above" in every sense, from His creation.

Reality consists only of God, and all of His creation.

Everything that exists came into being by the power and sovereign will of the infinite, personal God of the Bible. *Elohim*, the Almighty God, is the designer behind "intelligent design". He is the one who brought into being all plants, animals, fish, geography, elements, chemicals, natural laws, stars and planets, et al.

In the beginning God created the heavens . . .

CREATED LIFE AND BEING are bound by the dimension of time and space. The heavens, i.e. space, is the expanse in which the Creator placed the world, the planets, and the rest of the universe.

> Thou, even thou, art Lord alone; thou hast made heaven, the heaven of heavens, with all their host, the earth, and all things that are therein, the seas, and all that is therein, and thou preservest them all; and the host of heaven worshippeth thee (Nehemiah 9:6).

The expression, "the heavens", in the Hebrew of Genesis 1:1, *"Ha Shemayim"*, is plural. As the biblical revelation unfolds, we learn that there are three heavens, each containing the other.

First, the expression "heaven" refers to the atmosphere around the earth, where clouds and birds are seen.

> Nevertheless he left not himself without witness, in that he did good, and gave us rain from heaven, and fruitful seasons, filling our hearts with food and gladness (Acts 14:17).

Secondly, "heaven" refers to the expanse, which we call space, in which the planets and stars and galaxies are set.

> For the stars of heaven and the constellations thereof shall not give their light: the sun shall be darkened in his going forth, and the moon shall not cause her light to shine (Isaiah 13:10).

Finally, there is the highest heaven, the place where God's throne is and where He dwells. When Solomon dedicated the temple, he prayed repeatedly that in the variety of circumstances and trials the Jews should find themselves, that *"You would hear from heaven, your dwelling place . . ."* and deliver the people.

> Behold, the heaven and the heaven of heavens is the Lord's thy God, the earth also, with all that therein is (Deuteronomy 10:14).

In the beginning God created . . . the earth . . .

ALL CREATED LIFE AND existence is bound by three dimensions: Time, Space and Matter. We are all something, somewhere, and we all exist at some time. But we are not God, nor are we a "part of God". We can only be what God made us to be, (human, flesh and blood, mortal, male or female), and we can only exist when and where He placed us according to His pleasure.

In the New Testament, Paul told the Greek philosophers on Mars Hill, that God set the boundaries of time and place that we might best seek him,

> God that made the world and all things therein, seeing that he is Lord of heaven and earth, dwelleth not in temples made with hands; Neither is worshipped with men's hands, as though he needed any thing, seeing he giveth to all life, and breath, and all things; And hath made of one blood all nations of men for to dwell on all the face of the earth, and **hath determined the times before appointed, and the bounds of their habitation; That they should seek the Lord**, if haply they might feel after him, and find him, though he be not far from every one of us (Acts 17:24-27).

God created us. This implies his ultimate ownership of us, and our accountability to Him. This is why there is a "creation controversy". One doesn't need to be a theologian to perceive that if we were created by someone, we owe that person our worship, and accountability at the very least.

Recognizing reality means accepting the Creator/creation distinction, as well as the divinely set limits of time, space, and matter, as ordained by that Creator for our own good and His glory. He made us who we are, and set us where and when we exist. It is His definition of our humanity that counts because our very existence is owed to His good will.

> In the beginning God created the heavens and the earth. And the earth was without form, and void; and darkness was upon the face of the deep. And the Spirit of God moved upon the face of the waters. And God said, Let there be light: and there was light (Genesis 1:1-3).

And the earth was formless and void . . .

WHEN GOD CREATED ALL things, the earth was yet formless and void. Matter existed as a watery, shapeless mass, and would not be complete until the Creator separated it, gave form to it and made it habitable. The text did not say that the earth *". . . became formless and void",* as those who hold to variations of the "gap theory" believe, as if there were some catastrophe between Genesis 1:1 and Genesis 1:2.

The text simply tells us that when God created matter, it was originally in a formless state, waiting for His creative hand to give shape to it. Furthermore, our physical world was also created in a state of darkness, for it pleased God to shape, and energize the world in later stages of creation.

And darkness was upon the face of the deep . . .

THE DARKNESS IS AN amoral reference; there is nothing evil about this darkness. Isaiah tells us that God *"forms the light and creates darkness"(45:7).* The deep refers to the unformed waters. Proverbs 8 tells us that God's wisdom *"set a compass upon the deep"* to give form to the waters that He had created.

And the Spirit of God moved upon the waters . . .

THE SPIRIT OF GOD moved across the waters. The Spirit is personal and active in the creative process. He moves, back and forth over the waters. The Hebrew word for Spirit, is *Ruach,* and is the same as the word for wind. The same holds for the word for spirit, *pneuma,* in the Greek New Testament. Spirit and wind are the same words. Jesus likened the in-finite, personal Holy Spirit to the wind in John 3.

> Marvel not that I said unto thee, Ye must be born again. The wind bloweth where it listeth, and thou hearest the sound thereof, but canst not tell whence it cometh, and whither it goeth: so is every one that is born of the Spirit (John 3:7-8).

The word in Genesis 1:3, for "moved" is translated "shake" in Jeremiah 23:9 and "flutters" in Deuteronomy 32:11. Morris in his commentary, *The Genesis Record*, makes an interesting observation on this point.

> In modern scientific terminology, the best translation would probably be "Vibrated". If the universe is to be energized, there must be an Energizer . If it is to be set in motion, there must be a Prime Mover . . . It is significant that the transmission of energy in the operations in the Cosmos is in the form of waves—light waves, heat waves, sound waves and so forth. . . . Waves are typically rapid back and forth movements and they are normally produced by the vibratory motion of a wave generator of some kind. Energy cannot create itself. It is most appropriate that the first impartation of energy to the universe is described as the "vibrating" movement of the Spirit of God himself. [4]

And God said, Let there be light; and there was light . . .

THE FIRST RECORDED WORDS of God are, **"Let there be Light!"** God speaks and by His creative word all things came into being.

The apostle John, in his epistle, reminded the disciples, *"This is the message we heard from him, and declare unto you, that God is light, and in Him is no darkness at all".* God, who is light, energized the world that He had created, by the words, "Let there be light".

Centuries later the psalmist would celebrate the creative power of God's Word.

> By the word of the Lord were the heavens made; and all the host of them by the breath of his mouth. He gathereth the waters of the sea together as an heap: he layeth up the depth in storehouses. Let all the earth fear the Lord: let all the inhabitants of the world stand in awe of him. For

he spake, and it was done; he commanded, and it stood fast (Psalm 33:6-9).

The apostle Paul would later compare the *"Let there be light"* of God in creation, with the New Creation, the redemptive work of the Word of God in the heart of fallen man.

For God, who commanded the light to shine out of darkness, hath shined in our hearts, to give the light of the knowledge of the glory of God in the face of Jesus Christ (2 Corinthians 4:6).

It should also be noted that the speaking forth of light, precedes the creation of sun and stars. In other words, there was light before the sun. Thus the sun is not the true light; rather the SON is the true light of the world.

After Creation comes a process of separation and definition.

And God said, Let there be light: and there was light. And God saw the light, that it was good: and God divided the light from the darkness. And God called the light Day, and the darkness he called Night. And the evening and the morning were the first day. And God said, Let there be a firmament in the midst of the waters, and let it divide the waters from the waters. And God made the firmament, and divided the waters which were under the firmament from the waters which were above the firmament: and it was so. And God called the firmament Heaven. And the evening and the morning were the second day (Genesis 1:3-7).

GOD THEN COMMENCED HIS WORK of division; dividing the

light from the darkness, thus creating days. The Creation would take six literal days, a day consisting of *"evening and morning".* By repeating the expression, "evening and morning" the Creator is drawing our attention to the fact that these are literal days as we know them.

In God's reckoning of a day, evening comes first, then morning. Holidays in the Jewish calendar commenced at evening, so also the Sabbath. In the creational pattern of evening and morning, we see shades of what the pslmist sang of, when he exulted, that *Weeping endures for the night, but joy comes in the morning . . .* (Psalm 30).

That evening comes first, then morning, reflects a wider truth, that darkness precedes the light; in creation, salvation, and even eschatologically. All was darkness, even in creation, until God spoke, "LIGHT BE!", diffusing all with light. Clarity and form took place, and the Creation began to teem with life.

Spiritually, fallen man is said to abide in darkness, moral and spiritual, until the light of God breaks through to his soul. In Jesus, *"the True light now shineth"*, for all who have received the Word of life and light.

And at the end of man's time on earth, on the "Day of the LORD", comes a period of darkness, a time of tribulation so intensely dark, that Jesus warned us,

> And there shall be signs in the sun, and in the moon, and in the stars; and upon the earth distress of nations, with perplexity; the sea and the waves roaring; Men's hearts failing them for fear, and for looking after those things which are coming on the earth: for the powers of heaven shall be shaken (Luke 21:25-26).

But all of earth's tribulation and gloom is to be followed by the breaking of a glorious new day, in which the Lord promises,

> But unto you that fear my name shall the Sun of
> righteousness arise with healing in his wings; and
> ye shall go forth, and grow up as calves of the stall
> (Malachi 4:2).

On the second day, the Creator continued His work of separation, by dividing the waters above, from the waters beneath. He did so, once again by divine command. **"Let there be a firmament in the midst of the waters . . ."** The Hebrew word "firmament", *raqia,* means an expanse, or a spread out area.

The separation of the waters involved placing water on earth and waters in a canopy over the atmosphere, i.e. *the firmament.* The waters below would become the salt and fresh water systems, necessary to sustain life. The waters above would be for a canopy of protection, creating greenhouse conditions for life.

In the separation of the waters also, there are shades of the end, dimly perceived at the beginning. In typology, the waters are a metaphor for the nations, as seen in later Scriptures.

> The Lord reigneth, he is clothed with majesty;
> the Lord is clothed with strength, wherewith he
> hath girded himself: the world also is stablished,
> that it cannot be moved. Thy throne is established
> of old: thou art from everlasting. **The floods have
> lifted up, O Lord, the floods have lifted up their
> voice; the floods lift up their waves.** The Lord on
> high is mightier than the noise of many waters,
> yea, than the mighty waves of the sea. Thy testi-
> monies are very sure: holiness becometh thine
> house, O Lord, for ever (Psalm 93:1-5).

> But the wicked are like the troubled sea, when
> it cannot rest, whose waters cast up mire and
> dirt. There is no peace, saith my God, to the wicked
> (Isaiah 57:20-21).

At the end, God shall again divide the waters of humanity, taking some above and sending others below in the final judgment of all men.

<> <> <>

And God said, Let the waters under the heaven be gathered together unto one place, and let the dry land appear: and it was so. And God called the dry land Earth; and the gathering together of the waters called he Seas: and God saw that it was good. And God said, Let the earth bring forth grass, the herb yielding seed, and the fruit tree yielding fruit after his kind, whose seed is in itself, upon the earth: and it was so. And the earth brought forth grass, and herb yielding seed after his kind, and the tree yielding fruit, whose seed was in itself, after his kind: and God saw that it was good. And the evening and the morning were the third day (Genesis 1:9-13).

ON THE THIRD DAY of Creation, God separated the earth from the waters, by gathering the waters, and raising up the great continents in whatever form they once were before the Flood.

Henry Morris gives us an idea of the complex activities that this powerful fiat of the Creator activated.

Tremendous chemical reactions got under way, as dissolved elements precipitated and combined with others to form the vast complex of minerals and rocks making the solid earth—its crust, its mantle and its core ... great earth movements also got underway, in response to differential heating and other forces. Finally the surface of solid earth appeared above the waters and an intricate net-

work of channels and reservoirs opened up on
the crust to receive the waters retreating off of the
rising continents. [5]

This activity is called in other parts of Scripture, "laying
the foundations of the earth. The prophet Job learned, while
under some heavy questioning by the Most High, that the
"Sons of God", i.e. angels, were joyful witnesses of this awesome spectacle.

> Where wast thou when I laid the foundations
> of the earth? declare, if thou hast understand-
> ing. Who hath laid the measures thereof, if thou
> knowest? or who hath stretched the line upon
> it? Whereupon are the foundations thereof fas-
> tened? or who laid the corner stone thereof; When
> the morning stars sang together, and all the sons
> of God shouted for joy? (Job 38:4-8).

I love it! The thought of the newly created angels seeing such majesty and power, and singing and shouting for
sheer joy! God, how awesome you are! There is no one at
all like You! Truly we sing with trembling lips the everlasting anthem, *Thou art worthy O Lord, to receive glory and
honor and power, for thou hast created all things and for thy
pleasure they are created, Thou Art worthy OH Lord!!!*

The emergence of the great land mass from out of the
waters on the third day of Creation, points also to the resurrection of Jesus on the third day of the New Creation, after
He had died for the sins of all men. Jesus death is depicted
as a drowning in some of the Psalms.

> Save me, O God; for the waters are come in unto
> my soul. I sink in deep mire, where there is no
> standing: I am come into deep waters, where the
> floods overflow me. I am weary of my crying: my
> throat is dried: min eyes fail while I wait for my
> God (Psalm 69:1-3).

The resurrection of the Messiah, is depicted as being "rescued out of many waters", by King David in Psalm 18.

> He reached down from on high and took hold of me; he drew me out of deep waters. He rescued me from my powerful enemy, from my foes, who were too strong for me. They confronted me in the day of my disaster, but the Lord was my support. He brought me out into a spacious place; he rescued me because he delighted in me (Psalm 18:16-20).

Over the newly set foundations, God had carpeted the earth with various soils, brimming with everything needed for the development and nourishment of plant, animal and most importantly, human life.

Then the Creator, spoke again. He called out of the soil, all vegetation, grass, herb yielding seed, and reproducing fruit trees. The emphasis is that all vegetation bore seed, which could reproduce after its own kind. These plants were not seeds, but were created in full maturity, bearing seed within themselves.

God created a complete and mature creation. Adam was a full-grown man when he was created. These trees were created with fruit already on them. Later, animals would come along created as mature beasts. There was no slow development, rather, He spoke and all came into being. The third day was the beginning of life on earth, as the "third day" would one day become the basis for new life on earth.

All is being prepared, with meticulous care for our habitation. The Creator patiently puts all in place, as for a guest; a beautiful garden, nourishing food, perfect temperature, clean water, beauty for the eyes of the ones favored to dwell there. But God does all of the work Himself. There will be nothing that the favored guests could ever add to, or take away from the loving provision of God.

<> <> <>

And God said, Let there be lights in the firmament of the heaven to divide the day from the night; and let them be for signs, and for seasons, and for days, and years: And let them be for lights in the firmament of the heaven to give light upon the earth: and it was so. And God made two great lights; the greater light to rule the day, and the lesser light to rule the night: he made the stars also. And God set them in the firmament of the heaven to give light upon the earth, And to rule over the day and over the night, and to divide the light from the darkness: and God saw that it was good. And the evening and the morning were the fourth day (Genesis 1:14-19).

GOD CREATED LIGHT ON the first day, but the sun and moon and stars on the fourth day. The difference is that on the first day, God said, *"Let there be light"*, literally **Or**. But on the fourth day, God said let there be *"lights"*, or *"light givers"*, i.e. **Ma-Or.**

The Creator, made two main lights, "the greater light", (the sun) to rule the day and "the lesser light", to rule the night. Of course this account of Creation is given from a geo-centric perspective. The sun and moon are essential, the stars incidental for light. The sun was created as a light generator, the moon as a light reflector.

In John's account of the New Creation, in the Gospel of John, this same distinction of lights is made, contrasting the "True Light", i.e. Jesus the incarnated Word of God, with John the Baptist, or with any human witness to the Word of God,

There was a man sent from God, whose name was John. The same came for a witness, to bear witness of the Light, that all men through him might believe. He was not that Light, but was sent to bear witness of that Light. That was the true Light, which lighteth every man that cometh into the world (John 1:6-9).

The church is a light, but only a reflected light. We are true witnesses only to the extent that we reflect the light of God. We lose our capacity to reflect light when we turn away or even drift away from God. Jesus the LORD is the only true self-generating light of the world, penetrating the darkness of sin and estrangement from God.

These celestial lights were to be for "signs and seasons" as well as to measure days and years. But what were they to be signs of? History has indeed been marked by celestial portents of great events.

There are those who speculate that the 12 constellations now known as the Zodiac were a teaching of some kind. However, since the Fall of man, we are no longer able to properly interpret the "signs in the stars" because of the corruption of our reason and our tendency towards idolatry. Therefore God has forbidden any form of stargazing, or astrology.

Stand now with thine enchantments, and with the multitude of thy sorceries, wherein thou hast laboured from thy youth; if so be thou shalt be able to profit, if so be thou mayest prevail. Thou art wearied in the multitude of thy counsels. **Let now the astrologers, the stargazers, the monthly prognosticators, stand up, and save thee from these things that shall come upon thee. Behold, they shall be as stubble; the fire shall burn them;** they shall not deliver themselves from the power of the flame: there shall not be a coal to warm at, nor fire to sit before it. Thus shall they be unto thee with whom thou hast laboured, even thy merchants, from thy youth: they shall wander every one to his quarter; none shall save thee (Isaiah 47:12-15).

There is a legitimate scientific study of astronomy, which reveals that the starry heavens operate on a massive scale of time, space and matter, with a precision that would make a Swiss watch look primitive. Billions of stars, planets, galaxies, covering billions and trillions of miles interact daily in a precise manner.

Yet all is perfectly in order; comets travel with regularity in orbits that can be anticipated in intervals of years. Laws govern the circuits of massive heavenly bodies, which allow them to be studied and predicted. Scientists have discovered that if the earth were not shielded by Jupiter and Saturn we would have long ago been pelted with meteors and comets and would not be able to sustain life.[6]

There are heavenly bodies that absolutely dwarf the earth. They could contain thousands of earths, and whose gravitational pull could suck the earth into themselves from millions of miles away! But the earth is perfectly situated to teem with life. Were it any closer to the sun, we would burn up, any further we would freeze over. The position of the earth in the Milky Way Galaxy is ideal.

The built-in features of the earth—such as the perfectly tilted axis, the rotational lift, our magnetic field which serves as a meteor and radiation shield, and our moon—all cry out as a witness to the Intelligent and Loving Designer, who surely created this planet, among the trillions of other celestial objects, as a habitation for us.

> O Lord, our Lord, how excellent is thy name in all the earth! who hast set thy glory above the heavens. Out of the mouth of babes and sucklings hast thou ordained strength because of thine enemies, that thou mightest still the enemy and the avenger. When I consider thy heavens, the work of thy fingers, the moon and the stars, which thou hast ordained; What is man, that thou art mindful of him? and the son of man, that thou visitest

him? For thou hast made him a little lower than the angels, and hast crowned him with glory and honour. Thou madest him to have dominion over the woks of thy hands; thou hast put all things under his feet: All sheep and oxen, yea, and the beasts of the field; The fowl of the air, and the fish of the sea, and whatsoever passeth through the paths of the seas. O Lord our Lord, how excellent is thy name in all the earth! (Psalm 8).

<> <> <>

THE TIME HAD COME by the fifth day, to bring forth conscious animal life.

> *And God said, Let the waters bring forth abundantly the moving creature that hath life, and fowl that may fly above the earth in the open firmament of heaven. And God created great whales, and every living creature that moveth, which the waters brought forth abundantly, after their kind, and every winged fowl after his kind: and God saw that it was good. And God blessed them, saying, Be fruitful, and multiply, and fill the waters in the seas, and let fowl multiply in the earth. And the evening and the morning were the fifth day (Genesis 1:20-23).*

The fifth day of Creation is unique. By the power of His Word, God filled and covered the earth and the seas with animal life. In fact, this is the first mention of life, the Hebrew word *nephesh* meaning both *life* and *soul*. Plants are a form of life, but they don't have *nephesh*, i.e., soul, or consciousness, as animals and men do.

God called forth every kind of animal life, on earth, in the seas and rivers and in the upper and lower atmosphere of the sky. He saw the living creatures He had made, and pronounced them as "good". God then pronounced a blessing/decree to all animal life, to be fruitful and fill the earth.

> *And God said, Let the earth bring forth the living creature after his kind, cattle, and creeping thing, and beast of the earth after his kind: and it was so. And God made the beast of the earth after his kind, and cattle after their kind, and every thing that creepeth upon the earth after his kind: and God saw that it was good (Genesis 1:24-25).*

In what seems to be a threefold division of animal life, the earthbound animals are described as "cattle", "creeping things", and beasts. "Cattle" would seem to correspond to domestic animals, "creeping things", to insects, small rodents and reptiles, and finally "beasts" would refer to wild animals of all kinds. All of these were made instantaneously and simultaneously.

God saw this all as good. Furthermore, they were each made after their own kind. There would be no evolving from one species to the other.

Psalm 104, which is a celebration of Creation, portrays the animals as being dependent upon God from day-to-day, looking to the Creator for each meal, for drink also, and for their homes and even for their bedtime.

> He sendeth the springs into the valleys, which run among the hills. They give drink to every beast of the field: the wild asses quench their thirst. By them shall the fowls of the heaven have their habitation, which sing among the branches. He watereth the hills from his chambers: the earth is satisfied with the fruit of thy works. He causeth the grass to grow for the cattle, and herb for the service of man: that he may bring forth food out of the earth; . . .

> The trees of the Lord are full of sap; the cedars of Lebanon, which he hath planted; Where the birds make their nests: as for the stork, the fir trees are her house. The high hills are a refuge for the wild goats; and the rocks for the conies. He appointed the moon for seasons: the sun knoweth his going down. Thou makest darkness, and it is night: wherein all the beasts of the forest do creep forth. **The young lions roar after their prey, and seek their meat from God.** The sun ariseth, they gather themselves together, and lay them down in their dens (Psalm 104).

As another Psalm portrays, *"The eyes of all look to you, Oh Lord"* (Psalm 145).

How beautiful and harmonious the original plan for man and beast must have been. Even in its fallen state, the living creatures of the earth are stunning in their beauty and variety! We marvel as we watch the modern nature documentaries, and see the handiwork of the Creator on full display.

To behold the majesty of the lion, the grace and speed of a horse, the resourcefulness of squirrels and raccoons, the usefulness of the ox, the stunning beauty in sight and sound of birds, just to mention a few of God's creatures, all testifing to the beauty of God Himself.

We wait for the day when finally, the primal curse of vanity is lifted from the earth, and all of creation bursts out with joy at the liberation wrought by the Savior/Creator, and when the fear and enmity which marks the animal world will be removed forever, **for Creation itself shall be delivered from the bondage of corruption into the glorious liberty of the children of God** (Romans 8:21).

> The wolf also shall dwell with the lamb, and the leopard shall lie down with the kid; and the calf and the young lion and the fatling together; and a little child shall lead them. And the cow and the

bear shall feed; their young ones shall lie down together: and the lion shall eat straw like the ox. And the sucking child shall play on the hole of the asp, and the weaned child shall put his hand on the cockatrice' den. They shall not hurt nor destroy in all my holy mountain: for the earth shall be full of the knowledge of the Lord, as the waters cover the sea (Isaiah 11:6-9).

By now all was ready for the creation of man, the one for whom all else had been so painstakingly prepared.

And God said, Let us make man in our image, after our likeness: and let them have dominion over the fish of the sea, and over the fowl of the air, and over the cattle, and over all the earth, and over every creeping thing that creepeth upon the earth. So God created man in his own image, in the image of God created he him; male and female created he them.

<> <> <>

And God blessed them, and God said unto them, Be fruitful, and multiply, and replenish the earth, and subdue it: and have dominion over the fish of the sea, and over the fowl of the air, and over every living thing that moveth upon the earth. And God said, Behold, I have given you every herb bearing seed, which is upon the face of all the earth, and every tree, in the which is the fruit of a tree yielding seed; to you it shall be for meat. And to every beast of the earth, and to every fowl of the air, and to every thing that creepeth upon the earth, wherein there is life, I have given every green herb for meat: and it was so. And God saw every thing that he had made,

and behold it was very good. And the evening and
the morning were the sixth day (Genesis 1:26-31).

NOTICE THAT RATHER THAN the command *"let the earth bring
forth . . ."* as in the earlier days of Creation, God speaks in a
much more personal manner, among Himself, in the Godhead. ***"Let us make man in our image . . ."***

Obviously, to God, there is something special about man.
The way He created him is utterly unique to all of the rest
of creation. All that preceded him was a preparation before
him, for man is the pinnacle of creation. Man alone was created to bear the image and likeness of his Creator, and to
him only, was there granted a conscious fellowship with the
Godhead.

His first command was to *"be fruitful and multiply."*
This commandment is something God has never revoked,
though man has since fallen. God wants us to have children
and to fill the earth with them. Obviously, He wants us to be
saved and to raise the children in the fear and teaching of
the Lord, but God has never regarded children as anything
but a blessing.

Man has been called to be the vice-regent of God, ruling over all of the animals and developing, cultivating and
husbanding the many resources that God in His goodness
and wisdom has put into the earth, to be sought, extracted,
developed and enjoyed by man.

Man is not an animal, though with his feet firmly planted on the ground, and having been made also of the dust of
the earth, and depending entirely on vegetation for his sustenance, as the animals do, there is an affinity with animals.

But man can speak. He is self-conscious and aware. He
has been created with the capacity to commune with God,
and to long for eternity. Man is something more than a beast.

What is man, that thou art mindful of him? and

the son of man, that thou visitest him? For thou
hast made him a little lower than the angels, and
hast crowned him with glory and honour. Thou
madest him to have dominion over the works
of thy hands; thou hast put all things under his
feet: All sheep and oxen, yea, and the beasts of the
field; The fowl of the air, and the fish of the sea,
and whatsoever passeth through the paths of the
seas. O Lord our Lord, how excellent is thy name
in all the earth! (Psalm 8:4-9).

What is the image of God? God speaks, and so does man.
Man is creative, and conscious of eternity. He is responsible
for his actions. He can choose. He thinks abstractly. He is not
guided by instinct or appetite. He is a rational, moral being.
Furthermore, like God, man has been given an eternal spirit.

Remember that we are let into the very councils of God.
In Genesis 1, we overhear the Godhead commune within itself, saying, *"Let us make man in our image".* God cannot be
truly known other than as a Trinity of persons, Father, Son
and Holy Spirit.

Man, the image of God, in a faint, diminished way is also
created as a trinity: spirit, soul and body. By the spirit of
man, comes the capacity to worship, to long for God and
eternity, to respond in faith and love to the Creator.

The spirit expresses itself through the soul of man, i.e.,
the mind, will and emotions, as well as the conscience. Finally the spirit/soul of man, (the inner man) communicates
in this physical world through the body.

The believer in Jesus is promised a complete salvation.

And the very God of peace sanctify you wholly; and
I pray God your whole spirit and soul and body be
preserved blameless unto the coming of our Lord
Jesus Christ. Faithful is he that calleth you, who
also will do it (1 Thessalonians 5:23-24).

Man is still considered to be in the image of God after the Fall, but in some sense that image is marred and shattered by sin. The reason given for the death penalty for murderers is because those who kill destroy the image of God.

> Whoso sheddeth man's blood, by man shall his blood be shed: for in the image of God made he man (Genesis 9:6).

Salvation involves the restoration of the shattered image, through the Son of God, Jesus, who is the true image of the invisible God.

> And have put on the new man, which is renewed in knowledge after the image of him that created him (Colossians 3:10).

BLESSED GOD, RESTORE WITHIN us the image of You that we have shattered, through the name and work of Jesus Christ, our Lord!

2

For Man: Rest, a Garden, a Task, Freedom, and Marriage

> *Thus the heavens and the earth were finished, and all the host of them. And on the seventh day God ended his work which he had made; and he rested on the seventh day from all his work which he had made. And God blessed the seventh day, and sanctified it: because that in it he had rested from all his work which God created and made. These are the generations of the heavens and of the earth when they were created, in the day that the Lord God made the earth and the heavens (Genesis 2:1-4).*

THE SEVENTH DAY OF Creation has a blessing on it, which is "Rest". Furthermore, God has sanctified it. That is to say, it was set apart from all other days of the week. On the seventh day God rested from His work. Thus the Creator established a seven-day cycle of life for man, six days to labor, but the seventh to rest.

The concept of rest included the idea of completion. God's creation was accomplished, and He saw that it was good, and it was done. Henry Morris points out that whatever is happening in the universe since the original seventh day, falls into the category of either conservation or disintegration, in accordance with the two laws of thermodynamics. But it isn't creation, for Creation was completed on the seventh day.

> The present processes of the universe . . . are conservation and disintegration, as formulated in the two laws of thermodynamics. The processes of the creation period were processes of innovation and integration, ("creating" and "making"). Science can deal only with present processes, to which alone it has access.[7]

Man was made on the sixth day, as the very pinnacle of creation. Therefore his first full day was on the seventh, the day of rest. Thus, there was nothing that man could add to what God had done. It was for him (man) to begin his life on the day of rest, enjoying God's complete creation, without striving for anything. Out of his rest, the man was to accomplish his calling.

In other words, he is not trying to accomplish or attain to a position. He begins life already in the position of rest, as God's son and vice regent. This is grace.

So, also, it is in the new creation. It was only after the Lord said "It is finished", that our salvation could be accomplished, and that we could enter into a forgiven relationship with God.

In the New Testament concept, the Sabbath is a person. Jesus *"sat down"* at the right hand of God, after He had *"by himself purged our sins"*.   The believer is like Adam, who began life on the seventh day, after the work of creation was already done. So we also are saved not by our works, but by the work of Jesus. There is nothing we must do but by faith enter into the rest that He has purchased for us.

What a unique day that original Sabbath was! On that golden day, all was right in the world. Everything was complete and all of creation shared in "the rest" of God, enjoying complete harmony and the sense of fullness and satisfaction that the Hebrews call *shalom*.

Alas, "the Rest" was disturbed by sin soon afterwards, and the majority of mankind has failed to enter into anything like that wonderful sense of God-ordained rest since then. Spiritually, man is restless and miserable, like the mad man in Mark chapter 5, dwelling among the tombs, and crying day and night. Truly the prophet said, *"There is no peace for the wicked!"*

The story of Salvation is nothing less than the Creator working once again, making a righteous way to bring sinners back into the *shalom* intended for them, through the sacrifice of Jesus.

> Let us therefore fear, lest, a promise being left us of entering into his rest, any of you should seem to come short of it. For unto us was the gospel preached, as well as unto them: but the word preached did not profit them, not being mixed with faith in them that heard it. For we which have believed do enter into rest, as he said, As I have sworn in my wrath, if they shall enter into my rest: although the works were finished from the foundation of the world (Hebrews 4:1-3).

The New Testament Book of Hebrews takes this theme up again, reminding us that now, through Jesus, the way back into the Rest is restored. But we must "strive" by faith to enter into the rest of God .

> For he spake in a certain place of the seventh day on this wise, And God did rest the seventh day from all his works. And in this place again, If they shall enter into my rest. Seeing therefore

it remaineth that some must enter therein, and they to whom it was first preached entered not in because of unbelief: Again, he limiteth a certain day, saying in David, To day, after so long a time; as it is said, To day if ye will hear his voice, harden not your hearts. For if Jesus (Joshua) had given them rest, then would he not afterward have spoken of another day. There remaineth therefore a rest to the people of God. For he that is entered into his rest, he also hath ceased from his own works, as God did from his.

That God Himself rested on the seventh day, implies that "rest" in this sense has little or nothing to do with being tired. God's rest is a state of being. It is being right with God, free of sin, able to exult in God Himself and to rejoice in the work of another, that is, Christ, who tells us

Come unto me, all ye that labour and are heavy laden, and I will give you rest. Take my yoke upon you, and learn of me; for I am meek and lowly in heart: and ye shall find rest unto your souls. For my yoke is easy, and my burden is light (Matthew 11:28-30).

<> <> <>

... in the day that the Lord God made the earth and the heavens, And every plant of the field before it was in the earth, and every herb of the field before it grew: for the Lord God had not caused it to rain upon the earth, and there was not a man to till the ground. But there went up a mist from the earth, and watered the whole face of the ground. And the Lord God formed man of the dust of the ground, and breathed into his nostrils the breath of life; and man became a living soul (Genesis 2:4b-7).

THE SECOND CHAPTER OF Genesis revisits the Creation, especially that of plants, herbs, trees and man. The plants were not sustained by rain, nor were they yet tended or cultivated by anyone, but were watered by means of a subterranean misting system. With the Lord's provision of plants for food, shade, and for beauty, all was now in readiness for the creation of the man.

In Genesis one, we are told that *God (Elohim) created man in His own image,* but the account in Genesis two is more personal and intimate. Throughout the second chapter we are given the covenant personal name of the Creator—*The LORD God, (YHWH Elohim) formed man of the dust of the ground.*

Furthermore, He is "hands on" in the forming of man's body. Working with the dirt that He had already created, the Master Craftsman forms for the man a perfect body, getting His hands dirty in the process.

Finally, the divine intimacy in the forming of the man is expressed in the way He infused and animated Adam, breathing into his nostrils the very breath of life! Who do you ever allow to literally breath into your mouth or nostrils? How close would you have to be to someone for him or her to do so? The mighty God could have just as easily created man by fiat alone, but His interest in us is such that He reveals His full name, gets His hands dirty, and literally does a form of "mouth to mouth, or nose" to bring us to life. No wonder the psalmist pondered,

> When I consider thy heavens, the work of thy fingers, the moon and the stars, which thou hast ordained; **What is man, that thou art mindful of him? and the son of man, that thou visitest him?** For thou hast made him a little lower than the angels, and hast crowned him with glory and honour (Psalm 8:3-5).

Many centuries later, God would once again breathe the breath of life upon some, as an act of New Creation, after He had by Himself made the way for us to be reconciled to Himself and to be reborn by the Spirit of life in Christ.

> Then said Jesus to them again, Peace be unto you: as my Father hath sent me, even so send I you. And when he had said this, he breathed on them, and saith unto them, Receive ye the Holy Ghost: Whose soever sins ye remit, they are remitted unto them; and whose soever sins ye retain, they are retained (John 20:21-23).

Thus, by the mercy of the LORD God, man became a living soul.

Man is something of the earth, because he was formed by the dust of the earth, and resonated with the earthly. But he also has a consciousness; that is a soul, which can reason, imagine, communicate, and talk. He has a will, perception, mind and emotions. He is a free moral agent, a person bearing the image of God.

We were told that God had animated the animals as well, and they have souls (*nephesh*), but the animals were not formed with such divine, and personal care as man was. Man is different—he is earthy, but not an animal. He is something more than an animal.

By the infusion of the "breath of life", man was given something else that can distinguish him from animals, for he has been given spirituality—a capacity to know, enjoy, perceive and fellowship with the LORD God Himself on a level that none other in creation have been given. Eternity was put into his heart, according to the preacher in Ecclesiastes.

But the man would have a dependant life. The LORD God alone is self-existent, needing nothing, utterly sufficient in Himself, and is Himself the only source of life. Man would live by God. Only the Father and the Son have "life in themselves". All other life is dependant life. Should the man ever be separated from his God, he would also be separated from life itself, for God is our life.

> Verily, verily, I say unto you, The hour is coming, and now is, when the dead shall hear the voice of the Son of God: and they that hear shall live. For as the Father hath life in himself; so hath he given to the Son to have life in himself (John 5:25-26).

> And this is the record, that God hath given to us eternal life, and this life is in his Son. He that hath the Son hath life; and he that hath not the Son of God hath not life (1 John 5:11-12).

<> <> <>

And the Lord God planted a garden eastward in Eden; and there he put the man whom he had formed. And out of the ground made the Lord God to grow every tree that is pleasant to the sight, and good for food; the tree of life also in the midst of the garden, and the tree of knowledge of good and evil. And a river went out of Eden to water the garden; and from thence it was parted, and became into four heads . . . And the Lord God took the man, and put him into the garden of Eden to dress it and to keep it. And the Lord God commanded the man, saying, Of every tree of the garden thou mayest freely eat: But of the tree of the knowledge of good and evil, thou shalt not eat of it: for in the day that thou eatest thereof thou shalt surely die (Genesis 2:8-15).

GENESIS TWO RECOUNTS THE special care that the LORD God took in man's creation; personally fashioning the body of the man with His own hands, and breathing mouth to nostrils into the man the "breath of life", thus animating the first man, into a "living soul". In the same way, we see the personal, divine attention in the preparation of the appointed home of the first man, for God Himself planted a garden for man to dwell in.

The Garden was situated in a place named Eden, "Delight" or "Loveliness". As Erich Sauer said, **Paradise was the beginning of the ways of God with man here on earth**. The garden itself, was filled with handpicked trees, chosen for beauty and food, and was perfectly situated at the source for four rivers. (Was Eden on a mountaintop?) Truly the first home for humanity, was a "garden of delights", a place for the man to work, rest, eat and drink, in satisfaction. It was a spot selected by God for communion with the man, for God would take walks with the man and his wife, in the cool of the evening.

The man had been given a task. He was assigned by the Creator, to "dress and keep" the garden. Never has any man been so perfectly equipped to do so. The job of dressing and guarding the garden would involve all of man's God-given faculties: spirit, soul and body.

Adam lived a simple, threefold reality. His entire world consisted of God, himself and his surroundings, the garden. For the physical part of his task, Adam had been granted perfect senses: sight, smell, hearing, touch, and taste.

Mentally, Adam was created as a thinking, volitional person, possessing an unclouded intellect, and perfectly tuned emotions to deal with all that was abstract, and intellectual.

Spiritually, Adam was created to respond to His Creator. He alone of all creation was equipped to fully know, love, communicate with, and enjoy God.

Thus the first human, was so invested to fulfill the call on his life, to be the head of the race, to "be fruitful" and even to "subdue the earth", taking the dominion over all creatures, as the representative of God, bearing the image of God. Man was to be "ruler of the earth". His was a royal calling.

But first he must be given a smaller, preparatory task. He must simply dress and keep the garden. For the garden of delights was also a place of probation, that the man might be qualified by testing for greater responsibilities in God's purpose.

In the truest sense, and from the start, Adam was given freedom, *"Of every tree of the garden thou mayest freely eat . . .".* Freedom truly is man's natural and original state, for from the beginning, God gave Adam broad latitude; to eat anything he wanted, to have a family, a career, children, to rule, to live, laugh, and to worship God. No wonder the sons of Adam yearn to live in liberty.

But God didn't give Adam autonomy, i.e., unlimited liberty.

Adam and his wife were given one commandment. They were not to eat of the tree of the knowledge of good and of evil, on pain of death.

But of course the tree of the knowledge of good and evil wasn't walled off, or set somewhere remote and difficult to access. It stood in the garden for them to see every day.

If Adam would merely love God and believe His word, he would honor Him by not eating of the tree. The way for the first couple to show love, reverence and appreciation to God was to refrain from that one tree.

Martin Luther said of the tree,

> This tree of the knowledge of good and of evil was become Adam's altar and pulpit, from which he was to render due obedience to God, recognize God's word and will, and give him thanks. Had

Adam not fallen the tree would have been like a temple and cathedral!

The tree was the one sign of God's absolute authority, and Adam's loving, believing subjection to it. Every time he said "no" to any thought of eating of it, his inner life would be strengthened and deepened. His spiritual senses would have been trained to know from a position of "good", the ultimate Good, and to live by it, never knowing evil by experience.

The man was not intended to live alone however. The first "not good" in Creation occurred before the Fall of man, for it was "not good" for man to be alone. How do you turn a "not good" into a "good"?

<> <> <>

And the Lord God said, It is not good that the man should be alone; I will make him an help meet for him. And out of the ground the Lord God formed every beast of the field, and every fowl of the air; and brought them unto Adam to see what he would call them: and whatsoever Adam called every living creature, that was the name thereof. And Adam gave names to all cattle, and to the fowl of the air, and to every beast of the field; but for Adam there was not found an help meet for him. And the Lord God caused a deep sleep to fall upon Adam, and he slept: and he took one of his ribs, and closed up the flesh instead thereof; And the rib, which the Lord God had taken from man, made he a woman, and brought her unto the man. And Adam said, This is now bone of my bones, and flesh of my flesh: she shall be called Woman, because she was taken out of Man. Therefore shall a man

*leave his father and his mother, and shall cleave
unto his wife: and they shall be one flesh. And they
were both naked, the man and his wife, and were
not ashamed (Genesis 2:18-25).*

THE FIRST "NOT GOOD" pronounced by the LORD God on any
aspect of His creation, occurred before the Fall of man.
Therefore, it had nothing to do with Satan, sin or evil. God's
plan was not yet complete, for the LORD God had purposed
that man was not to be a solitary actor. It was not good that
the man was alone. God would make for him a help meet
(suitable and complimentary) for him.

This need for marital companionship was seemingly
underscored by the divinely assigned task of naming all of
the animals. Obviously, none of the beautiful creatures, as
unique and interesting as they were, could possibly meet
the need of the man for a life companion.

As Adam did the work of the first zoologist, naming and
classifying the animals as they paraded by him in their own
company, it became obvious that he needed a counterpart
also, someone he could relate to and share life with.

How does God turn a "not good" into a "Good"?

The LORD God did something about the problem that
looks a lot like death and resurrection.

God put Adam into a deep sleep, that He might perform
a kind of surgery upon him. The first human blood was shed
here, for God removed from the first man a side, (not a rib
as the KJV says), but a side in the Hebrew. He took a side out
of Adam's flesh, to form a woman from Adam's side. Then
the LORD God had to close up the flesh of Adam. (Was this
the first scar?)

The woman, who came out of Adam's side, was different from Adam, but she was complimentary to him. Both of
them comprise the image of God, for it is written, *"Male and*

female created He them in His Image . . .". But the woman was fashioned in a different and more refined way than the man. Man was formed out of the "dust of the earth", the soil. But woman was fashioned out of the side of man, refined and refashioned soil.

Even the order of Creation is significant. Man was created first, then woman. The woman was formed as a help suitable to the man. Centuries later when the apostle Paul was teaching the church, he referred to the order of Creation as a reason why leadership in the church should primarily be male.

> But I suffer not a woman to teach, nor to usurp authority over the man, but to be in silence. For Adam was first formed, then Eve (1 Timothy 2:12-13).

Men and women are equal but different, according to the Word of God. Gender is not a mere human construct, as the spirit of this evil age insists. Male and female are, in fact, God assigned roles, based upon the mode and order of Creation. The deliberate repudiation of these roles is one of the ultimate expressions of the world's final rebellion against God Himself.

Whatever a tormented soul does to his or her body in this evil generation cannot change the fact that every chromosome of his or her body remains either male or female as God created them. There is no true transsexual, only tormented and ruined eunuchs. These are the flotsam of our age's so-called "sexual revolution", anyone of whom, Jesus would forgive and heal with His love should they turn to Him.

As Adam came out of his deep sleep, he stood there before God, with the scar in his side, waiting to be presented by the LORD God, with the first woman—a creature of astonishing beauty and grace, no doubt.

This particular scene in the Scripture, foreshadows the final triumph, for the ultimate Groom also has a scar in His side, and awaits the time when the Father presents the Bride, the Lamb's wife, the body of the Messiah, the church, purchased by His blood.

<> <> <>

Adam said, This is now bone of my bones, and flesh of my flesh: she shall be called Woman, because she was taken out of Man. Therefore shall a man leave his father and his mother, and shall cleave unto his wife: and they shall be one flesh. And they were both naked, the man and his wife, and were not ashamed (Genesis 2:23-25).

THERE IS A WEDDING at very near the beginning of the Bible, and a wedding at the end of it. The union of man and wife is the fundamental human relationship. Before any other relationship—father/son, brother/brother, or brother/sister, friend/friend, employer/employee—the fundamental and primal relationship is husband/wife.

This first wedding is of prophetic significance, because the original groom, who had a scar in his side, from which his wife was taken, foreshadows the ultimate Bridegroom, Jesus, out of whose side blood and water poured forth when they pierced Him, whilst He was paying the price for His bridal church, (which He purchased from sin with His own blood).

Centuries later the apostle Paul would reveal to us by divine revelation, something of what Adam had been given a glimpse of on that hopeful day,

For this cause shall a man leave his father and

mother, and shall be joined unto his wife, and they two shall be one flesh. **This is a great mystery: but I speak concerning Christ and the church** (Ephesians 5:31-32).

The mystery of marriage is that it is, in itself, a sign that points to a greater reality—the love of the Messiah for His church. The word that God used when He said that He formed the woman out of Adam's side, is the same word that will be used to describe Cain building a city. We will see in Genesis chapter 4 that in rebellion against God, Cain built a city of rebellion. *Enoch*, (means "Inauguration"), a "New Start" without God, for all of those who wish to leave the presence of the Lord and to make their own life on their own terms.

But God has built a bride for Adam, and He has been building a bridal city for the Messiah, the Bride, the Lamb's wife, which is a "bridal city" of God,

> And there came unto me one of the seven angels which had the seven vials full of the seven last plagues, and talked with me, saying, Come hither, I will shew thee the bride, the Lamb's wife. And he carried me away in the spirit to a great and high mountain, and shewed me that great city, the holy Jerusalem, descending out of heaven from God, Having the glory of God: and her light was like unto a stone most precious, even like a jasper stone, clear as crystal (Revelation 21:9-11).

> Upon this rock I will build my church and the gates of hell will not prevail against it . . . (Matthew 16).

God Himself ordained marriage; it was not man's invention. Those who sin against marriage will give full account to God. To destroy a marriage is a deep, grievous sin, which God will require of all involved, for as the apostle who wrote

Hebrews reveals,

> Marriage is to be honored by all and whoremongers and adulterers, God will judge (Hebrews 13).

The Author of marriage is the unseen witness at every wedding, taking special note of the vows spoken in His presence. He is ever willing to give any couple the power to keep those vows, yet He will judge us on the basis of those vows.

What is marriage? The real Bridegroom defined it for us, when the Pharisees, who held a low view of marriage, questioned Him about the permissibility of divorce "for any reason". They cited a liberal interpretation of Moses' law of divorce. But Jesus would have none of that, instead taking them back "to the beginning".

> The Pharisees also came unto him, tempting him, and saying unto him, Is it lawful for a man to put away his wife for every cause? And he answered and said unto them, Have ye not read, that he which made them at the beginning made them male and female, And said, For this cause shall a man leave father and mother, and shall cleave to his wife: and they twain shall be one flesh? Wherefore they are no more twain, but one flesh. **What therefore God hath joined together, let not man put asunder** (Matthew 19:3-6).

Marriage is God taking two people and making of them "one flesh", one new person, with each retaining their individuality. Divorce is "putting them asunder", tearing them apart, which involves more than the tearing up of a piece of paper. It is literally the ripping apart of two joined together. This is why those who destroy marriage will answer to God in judgment.

"Leave your father and mother." In other words, all other relationships pale in comparison, even the closest ones (father and mother). Spiritually one must "leave one's parents" in order to be able to truly cleave to (cling, chase, adapt, adhere to) one's spouse.

The current assault on marriage is nothing less than satanic. It is because marriage is one of those divine institutions that is above all of us. It is sacred and the sodomites are compelled to seek to pull it down and profane it ("Gay marriage"), wiping their feet on it, to assure that there is nothing above them. But the God of marriage is taking names and making notes of the sacrilege.

3

The Serpent in the Garden

Now the serpent was more subtle than any beast of the field which the LORD God had made. And he said unto the woman, Yea, hath God said, Ye shall not eat of every tree of the garden? And the woman said unto the serpent, We may eat of the fruit of the trees of the garden: But of the fruit of the tree which is in the midst of the garden, God hath said, Ye shall not eat of it, neither shall ye touch it, lest ye die. And the serpent said unto the woman, Ye shall not surely die (Genesis 3:1-4).

HUMAN HISTORY BEGAN IN a garden of delight, Eden. God placed our first parents, Adam and Eve there.

God gave the man and woman but one commandment, a prohibition. They were commanded not to eat of the tree of the knowledge of good and of evil. A vast array of other beautiful, fruit bearing trees was theirs to enjoy at will.

We are told without explanation, that the snake spoke to the woman.

Now the serpent was subtle . . . but can a snake be subtle? Isn't subtlety a feature of intelligence? Subtlety is an attribute that can only be given to a responsible, moral being,

therefore the Scripture itself is being subtle, for it is imply-
ing that something more than a mere reptile is involved in
this story. The serpent is but the vehicle for another malev-
olent personality.

But something further is amiss, for in the fact that the
serpent spoke to the woman, there is rebellion against the
divine order. God had charged Adam with the commission
to "guard and keep" the garden. Adam was the one who
named the serpent, thus having authority over it. Why does
the serpent address the woman and not the man?

The method of the serpent's seduction of the first couple is enlightening. The serpent probed the understanding
of the woman, not by proposition but by loaded question.

> Yea, hath God said, Ye shall not eat of every tree of
> the garden?

What a masterpiece of insinuation! He neither affirms,
nor denies the Word of God, rather he calls God's principle
into question.

Yes, the serpent's question was certainly loaded. It
could be paraphrased: **Did God really deny you the freedom to eat of every tree of the garden?** Thus the serpent
insinuated that God's sole limit upon the couple was alto-
gether unreasonable.

The woman's response revealed the couple's inner
state; that perhaps there was some discontentment within
them to exploit.

> And the woman said unto the serpent, We may eat
> of the fruit of the trees of the garden: But of the
> fruit of the tree which is in the midst of the gar-
> den, God hath said, Ye shall not eat of it, neither
> shall ye touch it, lest ye die.

Notice that first, she maximized the prohibition of God,

(though not as greatly as the serpent), by saying that not only were they not to eat of the tree, they weren't even supposed to touch it! Thus she portrayed her benevolent Creator in a slightly harsh light, as though He was being unreasonable.

Secondly she minimized the divine sanction, telling the tempter that God had said, "... *lest ye die.*" What God had really said was, *"On the day you eat of the tree of the knowledge of good and evil, In dying you shall die!"* There was no ambiguity in God's word to Adam about it. Eve had misquoted God's word, denying the absolute surety of that portion of it.

By this time the serpent (correctly) perceived that the couple was prepared to hear God's Word openly denied. He would present them with an alternative "Word" of God.

<> <> <>

And the serpent said unto the woman, Ye shall not surely die: For God doth know that in the day ye eat thereof, then your eyes shall be opened, and ye shall be as gods, knowing good and evil (Genesis 3:4-5).

THE LIE OF THE serpent in the garden is the underlayment of all false religion, philosophy, psychology and the entire humanistic ideal that has so shaped our modern age. We see that the attraction to the Lie is stronger than ever before, and exerts a constant influence on education, law, medicine, the media, entertainment, literature and even popular religion.

What are the components of this pervasive and multi-faceted lie? Lets unpack it ...

You shall not surely die

The nature of death is that it is a punishment of God. Scripture declares in several places, that "the soul that sins . . . shall die", "It is appointed unto man once to die, and then the judgment", and that " The wages of sin is death . . .". This is what all men know instinctively and it is the aspect of death which men fear the most.

But the serpent's lie is a direct denial of all of the above. One out of seven people in the world believe in Hinduism, with its false doctrine of reincarnation, a direct echo of the serpent's lie. No wonder that false religion generally views the serpent positively, as the source of wisdom.

The cults are almost universal in their denial of the certainty and finality of death.

Buddhism teaches Nirvana, "nothingness", as the end of all men, a false hope that is catching on rapidly in the post-Christian West.

The serpent is currently hissing through neo evangelicals that "You shall not surely die", inspiring them to write books such as *Love Wins* by Rob Bell, which teach that God's love will not allow for a final, fiery judgment.

The ridicule and relegation of the doctrine of eternal punishment as being an outdated relic of a dark and bigoted past is just another form of the lie that *"you will not surely die"*. Satan doesn't want men to consider their own end.

. . . for God knows . . .

This aspect of the Lie is a direct assault on the goodness of God. The serpent would have men to believe that if there was a God, He is holding people back from something good, He is blocking their own self-realization. God supposedly knows something that would be satisfying and good for the couple but He withholds it for selfish reasons.

Satan has always wanted men to come to the conclusion that the God of the Bible with His laws and strictures has put men into bondage. Satan would liberate those in such bondage though.

> Why do the heathen rage, and the people imagine a vain thing? The kings of the earth set themselves, and the rulers take counsel together, against the Lord, and against his anointed, saying, Let us break their bands asunder, and cast away their cords from us (Psalm 2).

We are told in this, the second Psalm that this liberation movement has been taken up by the *"the kings of the earth and their rulers . . . against the Lord and His Anointed One".* The *"vain imagination"* they are enthralled with is that they can liberate millions of people from the *"Cords . . . and . . . bands"* of the LORD and of Christ.

Satan's lie echoes in the modern movement to do away with the bondage of Judeo-Christian religion, with its narrow definition of marriage, sexuality, gender, and strict moral code.

The day you eat of it, your eyes shall be opened

Supposedly, the serpent will be the one to enlighten you, to "open your eyes" to the secrets God has held back from you. This is the lie of the occult, the lure of "secrets", the "lost gospels", the hidden *gnosis* which eludes common people and simple-minded believers in God.

You shall be as gods

Here we come to the very heart of the Lie, that man can gain a knowledge, or undergo a mystical experience that will allow him to be as (a) god. What would it mean for you and I to be as gods? God has no limits. God is sovereign, independent and all-powerful. God makes His own rules. God answers to no one but Himself.

The primal, satanic lie has thoroughly leavened the world. One billion Hindus seek godhood as the goal and end of the burdensome cycle of reincarnation. Buddhists seek an enlightenment that will make them as the Dalai Lama, an "enlightened god". Mormonism's goal is the realization of personal godhood for its male adherents.

There are even heretical sects in Christianity, which propagate the serpent's lie, such as the Word of Faith movement, with its "Little Gods" teaching.

From the Tower of Babel onward, man is constantly erecting pyramids, ziggurats, step-by-step programs, and ever ascending degrees of initiation into some kind of oneness with Deity.

Usually it is the priests or emperors who are said to attain godhood, but the fact that there is any deified man, such as a pharaoh, a caesar, Dalai Lama or a pope, shows the rest of us the potential that lies within each of us. This is the logic of our constant "hero worship", and what underlies the current fascination with "super heroes".

Man projects onto his "stars", his own aspiration to be as a god. These are our celebrities, larger-than-life athletes, entertainers, political heroes, and religious figures. Thus, the Lie is ever affirmed, that mankind can ascend; he can indeed rise up to the level of God.

The "mystery of iniquity" is the New Testament term for this false belief, that man can rise up, and exalt self over God, and above all that is worshipped as god. This spiritual principle of human deification comes to its final climax in the emergence of the "man of sin", who is only the embodiment of all of the aspirations of the unbelieving world, which shall one day worship him.

> Who opposeth and exalteth himself above all that is called God, or that is worshipped; so that he as God sitteth in the temple of God, shewing himself that he is God ... For the mystery of iniquity doth already work ... (2 Thessalonians 2:4,7).

The divine counter to "the mystery of iniquity" lie, is something called in the New Testament, "the mystery of godliness". Can man evolve to the point of being exalted above god, beyond worship or fear itself? Can we ever "be as gods"? Never!

The problem is that the Truth that counters the Lie is less flattering. The fact that man is impotent, bankrupt and ruined by his fall into sin, is hard to swallow to the generation raised on humanistic optimism. Man can never be a god. If man is to be saved, God must become a man. God must descend to save us. God must come down to us in our low estate.

> And without controversy great is the mystery of godliness: **God was manifest in the flesh**, justified in the Spirit, seen of angels, preached unto the Gentiles, believed on in the world, received up into glory (1 Timothy 3:16).

> And no man hath ascended up to heaven, **but he that came down from heaven**, even the Son of man which is in heaven (John 3:13).

<> <> <>

> *When the woman saw that the tree was good for food, and that it was pleasant to the eyes, and a tree to be desired to make one wise, she took of the fruit thereof, and did eat, and gave also unto her husband with her; and he did eat (Genesis 3:6).*

> Wherefore, as by one man sin entered into the world, and death by sin; and so death passed upon all men, for that all have sinned ... (Romans 5:12).

RESPONSIBILITY FOR THE FALL of man is laid at the feet of Adam, the father of us all, not Eve. Never in all of the revelation of God, is she seen as being primarily the cause of the Fall. Adam was the person God called out immediately after the transgression, not Eve. Eve was deceived by the serpent, not Adam. The commission was given to Adam to guard and keep the garden.

Therefore it is interesting that the narrative of the Fall centers around the woman. The serpent approached the woman, accused God to her, and presented his arguments to her. We are told in verse 6 that Adam was there with her, but verse 6 is an account of her inner thoughts, which led to the transgression.

Is this not a warning that one of the telltale marks of the serpent is to marginalize the man from his God-assigned position of primal responsibility?

The modern feminist movement, is not really about femininity, but rather it is about the repudiation of the God-assigned gender roles, based upon hatred and envy of male status. Men, too, can be feminists, for it is a satanic philosophy, an expression of rebellion against God.

Feminism is actually the enemy of all that is truly feminine; the beauty of motherhood, tender nurture, fruitfulness, loving deference and submission for the greater good of the family, sacrifice of self for husband and children.

These are seen as impediments to the modern ideal woman, now "liberated" by abortion, and easy divorce. But liberated from what? Love? Stable marriage? Fruitfulness?

When Adam passively allowed his wife to take the lead in the couple's dealing with the serpent, by default he abdicated his high calling to keep and guard the garden of God. He had been given the Word, and the commission to have dominion over the earth, not Eve.

But through the serpent, Eve became the priest. It was Eve who mediated the serpent's false "Word", and she who "ministered" to Adam the "sacrament" (i.e., the forbidden fruit). Adam perversely took part in the sinful rite which was supposed to "open their eyes" and make them wise enough to become "as gods".

What we are seeing in the deliberate confusion of the gender roles today, even in the church, is the mark of satanic influence. Motherhood, and being a wife have been repudiated, in favor of "careerism". Female leadership in home and church is a denial of the divine order.

But wherever the confusion of gender is celebrated as a "liberating" accomplishment, homosexuality is never far behind. Note that the mainstream churches which once vigorously debated the ordination of women, by now have succumbed to the ordination of homosexuals.

The forbidden fruit was the knowledge of good and of evil.

To "know good and evil" is to know everything--the whole spectrum of knowledge. In fact to be "as gods, knowing . . ." is to have the ability to decide for yourself what good and evil are, thus to liberate yourself from dependence upon God and His Word.

We can see that by the time Eve paused to look at the tree, the Word of God had already been rejected by both of them, for her whole perspective is based on an inward acceptance of the Lie.

And when the woman saw that the tree was good for food

Who said that the tree was good for food? Not God! Not the Word of God, as given to Adam. God said *"that the day you eat of this tree . . . you will surely die . . ."*. But Eve could see (from her own vantage point), that the tree was good.

. . . and that it was pleasant to the eyes

In our vernacular, Eve thought, "It looks good to me." I have no doubt that the tree was pleasant to the eyes, but what does that have to do with what God had said about it?

But Eve was already acting on the serpent's promise that she and Adam could be *"as gods, knowing good and evil"* because she decided for herself what was good and what was evil. She had departed from the Word of God and was making her own judgments about the tree.

. . . and a tree to be desired to make one wise

But here is an indication that she really wasn't entirely as independent in her thoughts as she imagined, For this thought was entirely influenced by the lie of the serpent who was the only source for the idea that eating of the forbidden tree would make her "wise".

. . . she took of the fruit thereof . . . and did eat

Ages of pain, sorrow, disappointment and suffering hung in the balance of those few seconds it took for her to think through the temptation. But, as we all know, she reached out and took it, (in rebellion against her Maker).

She stretched out her hand, and took the fruit for herself, (self-improvement; it was the secret way to become wise!).

And she ate it.

It would be easy to assume that this is a story about Eve, because the Scripture focuses on Eve's thought processes, and on her sin. Adam's fall is reported almost incidentally to Eve's.

. . . and gave also unto her husband with her; and he did eat

But it was Adam's fall that was the goal. When Adam received the fruit from his wife, and ate it, the Fall of man occurred. That was the point at which death entered, and all of the pain, sorrow, death, disappointment, terror, fear, hurt, disease, futility—in short everything we experience as a direct or indirect result of sin—came into the world. All of humanity was counted "in Adam" and fell "in Adam".

> For since by man came death, by man came also
> the resurrection of the dead. For as in Adam all
> die, even so in Christ shall all be made alive (1
> Corinthians 15:21-22).

Paul would further assert that the disobedience of Adam has had a universal effect on all of mankind, so pervasive that there is only one effective counter to the "one offence" out of which all of human sin is but an outworking.

That would be what Paul refers to as the "obedience of the one" man, the Last Adam, the Second Man, Jesus Christ the Lord.

> Therefore as by the offence of one judgment came
> upon all men to condemnation; even so by the
> righteousness of one the free gift came upon all
> men unto justification of life. For as by one man's
> disobedience many were made sinners, so by the
> obedience of one shall many be made righteous
> (Romans 5:18-19).

<> <> <>

> *And when the woman saw that the tree was good*
> *for food, and that it was pleasant to the eyes, and*
> *a tree to be desired to make one wise, she took of*
> *the fruit thereof, and did eat, and gave also unto*
> *her husband with her; and he did eat (Genesis 3:6).*

THERE HAS LONG BEEN much confusion about the nature of Adam's sin. This is partly because it is hard for us to imagine how the simple act of plucking fruit from the forbidden tree could merit such devastating consequences, not only for Adam but for the entire human race.

Therefore people have speculated about what the "forbidden fruit" actually was. Was it the apple? Or was it the pomegranate? What fruit was it? What impact did eating it have on the first couple? Why was this simple act of disobedience of such dreadful import?

There are others who have applied figurative significance to the first transgression, saying that the fruit represented something else. Many believe that the forbidden fruit is a metaphor for human sexuality, and that it was in that fashion that Adam and Eve had their "eyes opened".

The Scriptures teach nothing of the sort. In fact, they teach the opposite. Adam and Eve were commanded by God from the beginning to "be fruitful and multiply". Therefore how could married intimacy be considered the sin that evicted them from the garden?

Satan has always sought to sully human marital intimacy, as being somehow "evil" or less than spiritual. This false teaching reinforces the original lie that God is keeping something wonderful from us, and implies that liberation comes by transgressing God's commands.

> Now the Spirit speaketh expressly, that in the latter times some shall depart from the faith, giving heed to seducing spirits, and **doctrines of devils**; Speaking lies in hypocrisy; having their conscience seared with a hot iron; **Forbidding to marry** . . . (1 Timothy 4:1-2).

Certainly, as we have learned by bitter and painful experience in the so-called "sexual revolution", Satan is not the "sexual liberator". Rather, his teaching leads to vast and intense social and personal destruction, perversion of life and character, and ultimately to hell itself. The sexual revolution has killed love and romance for millions, and degraded and ruined the lives of millions of its devotees. There is no love in the world of *Playboy*, only abortion, divorce, disenfranchisement, and misery.

The original transgression wasn't sexual. It certainly wouldn't have been wrong for Adam to "know his wife". The two being "one flesh" as husband and wife, was always part of the original plan and commission.

Neither did it matter which fruit was forbidden for the first couple, for the point wasn't that there is a "special fruit" off-limits to man but reserved for God alone.

Underneath every sinful act is a religious principle that is being called into question. Temptation forces us to choose one side or another, faith or unbelief, submission to God or autonomy, worship, or self-absorption.

The point of setting off one tree out of the thousands, and commanding Adam and Eve not to eat of it, had to do with loving trust, and loyalty to God. By refusing to eat of the tree, Adam and Eve were proclaiming to all of creation that they, the pinnacle of creation, chose to remain under God the Creator as worshippers.

The tree was a limit set by God, by which Adam and Eve could have daily proclaimed before all and sundry, "Not my will, O God, but thine be done", or "Not unto us O Lord, not unto us, but unto thy name give glory". It represented the sovereignty of God, the holiness of God, and not touching it demonstrated loving respect and reverence for God.

God would have had them to know good and evil by simple trust in His word to them, (the one commandment). They could have observed it out of a sense of grateful love. But when Satan challenged them to "know good and evil" for themselves, it was a call to personal experience of evil, based upon mistrust and false accusation of God.

Would Adam remain in a position of "exalted submission" under God, as a worshipper of God? Would he trust that God's way was the best way? Would Adam and Eve remain in love with the One who created them and favored them so greatly?

When Adam reached out his hand to eat the fruit for himself, in the process he trampled under his feet love for God, trust, commitment, loyalty and worship. He actually sided with the serpent, who had also rebelled against God, usurping God's very throne.

It was the principle of trust and love that was repudiated in the eating of the forbidden fruit. Taking that fruit was an act of rebellion. It was a rejection of God's rule over the couple, for it was a bid for autonomy. Adam no longer believed that God's way was the best way, or that he owed gratitude and worship to God. By taking the fruit for himself, he was proclaiming, "Not Thy will but mine be done!"

4

Fall and Estrangement

And the eyes of them both were opened, and they knew that they were naked; and they sewed fig leaves together, and made themselves aprons. And they heard the voice of the LORD God walking in the garden in the cool of the day: and Adam and his wife hid themselves from the presence of the LORD God amongst the trees of the garden (Genesis 3:7-8).

IMMEDIATELY AFTER THEY TRANSGRESSED, we are told that Adam and Eve became acutely aware of it. Their eyes were indeed opened, but not in the way that they had expected. Upon acting out their rejection of the Word of God, our first parents realized, to their own horror, that they had committed a kind of spiritual suicide.

They were enlightened all right, for they now knew by experience what death really is.

When the Creator told Adam that they would die the day they ate of the forbidden tree, Adam could only know death by revelation of God. He would have to take God's word for it that disobedience would bring death, and that death is not desirable. That should have been sufficient for the first couple.

But after allowing the serpent to seduce them into distrusting God, now they would know death by experience, for indeed on that very day, Adam and Eve died, and the human race died with them.

> Wherefore, as by one man sin entered into the world, and death by sin; and so death passed upon all men, for that all have sinned . . . For as by one man's disobedience many were made sinners, so by the obedience of one shall many be made righteous (Romans 5:12, 19).

It should be obvious that the death God warned of, is not limited to physical death, for Adam would continue to live for another 930 years. From the moment he transgressed, his own physical death was assured. But the couple would now know spiritual and moral death in all of its forms, for the rest of their now limited lives.

Death is more than a physical reality; it is a state of being. To die is to be "cut off" from the real source of our life. Death is estrangement from God.

The first couple now "knew that they were naked". They could sense their vulnerability. They had become self-conscious and painfully aware that no longer were they covered as before when they dwelt under God, in communion with Him and clothed in His glory.

From then on, the particular parts of the body which were intended for procreation, would be accompanied with a sense of shame, as though the high calling of God given to the first man and his wife to "be fruitful and multiply", had been affected.

Yes, the man and his wife were still called to bring forth the human race, but they would pass on to their seed their own estrangement from God the Creator. All who would come from the loins of Adam would also share in the corruption of his nature.

Because of Adam's disobedience, the beautiful calling of procreation and birth is now associated with the transmission of sin and death, therefore, generally speaking, humanity has an innate sense that the loins are to be covered.

No longer acting in accordance with the Word of God, the man and his wife began to act out of self volition. They were on their own, operating out of their own limited wisdom and (now) perverted perception.

Therefore Adam and Eve moved quickly to remedy this new-found sense of shame and nakedness, for they made themselves garments of fig leaves. This was the first expression of self-redemption—the erroneous attempt to deal with guilt and estrangement, by human effort.

This man-made religion, also known as "will worship", is the undergirding of all world religion, philosophy, and culture.

Self-redemption is the vain imagination that we can get things right without humble submission to God. All sons of Adam know universally that we are spiritually and morally naked, and that there is something wrong with us that needs to be set aright.

There are numerous examples of this, such as Hinduism's cycle of Karma and reincarnation, Islam's tortured works righteousness, the Buddhist "noble path", or even the works righteousness of Judaism and heretical Christianity. Consider the centuries of extreme renunciation and self-flagellation of monks such as Martin Luther.

All of these prove to be Adam's fig leaves. There is a deep instinct in all of us to "cover up" by self-redemption or reformation. But all fig leaves are inadequate to heal the breach between God and man, and the conscience knows it.

Adam and Eve, in the process of hiding their shame from God, also ended up hiding from each other. The personal estrangement would prove to be vertical and horizontal, death was working already.

The serpent told them they would "know good and evil", well, now evil was being revealed to Adam. He would learn immediately that sin, (evil) is divisive; it breaks fellowship and makes communion impossible. Death is separation.

Man became separated from God. He hid from Him whom he once walked with in the cool of the evening.

- The man and His wife were also separated, for they blamed each other, when accountability was demanded of them.

- The separation radiated outward as more men increased. For man in sin is alienated from all other men, thus human history is marked by wars, division, and murder.

- Man was separated from his environment, for the once-friendly ground became the weed-choked place of frustrating toil.

- Finally, Man was separated even from himself, for sin created psychological dissonance and contradiction. At the end, came the final indignity, man's soul would be separated from his body.

Lost, condemned and estranged, our first parents would not come to God . . . but God, in Genesis three, came to seek them out. That's what happened in the garden, and it was a picture of what would happen in history, God came to seek us out.

<> <> <>

And they heard the voice of the LORD God walking
in the garden in the cool of the day: and Adam and

*his wife hid themselves from the presence of the
LORD God amongst the trees of the garden. And
the LORD God called unto Adam, and said unto him,
Where art thou? And he said, I heard thy voice in
the garden, and I was afraid, because I was naked;
and I hid myself (Genesis 3:8-10).*

IN THE MOMENTS FOLLOWING the transgression, to their
horror, Adam and Eve experienced the ever-increasing ram-
ifications of sin. Sin is death. It is death to friendship, love
communion, trust, and peace . . . in short, to everything that
makes life beautiful.

Had they not sinned, the couple would have delighted
in fellowship with the LORD. But now, terror gripped their
hearts, as they heard the sound of the LORD God drawing
near to them.

Adam and Eve well knew that their sin had made them
guilty. It was not that they now felt guilty, but that having
sinned they were now truly guilty. They had transgressed,
and were now fully liable to divine judgment.

The prospect of standing naked and ashamed before the
Holy, benevolent God filled them with fear. God would see
them! He would look upon their nakedness and shame with
holy eyes; it was too much to bear.

Therefore they hid themselves, as the sons and daughters of Adam and Eve have been doing ever since. Guilty
man ever flees from his enemy, the Holy God, as it is written, *"there is none that seeketh after God . . . they have all
gone out of the way."*

This flight from the only true God, is an exercise in futility, because God is omnipresent, and omniscient, as the
psalmist reminds us.

Whither shall I go from thy spirit? or whither
shall I flee from thy presence? If I ascend up into

> heaven, thou art there: if I make my bed in hell,
> behold, thou art there. If I take the wings of the
> morning, and dwell in the uttermost parts of the
> sea; Even there shall thy hand lead me, and thy
> right hand shall hold me (Psalm 139:7-10).

But Adam's fallen instinct was to run from God, and to attempt to hide from Him. He was on his own, autonomous; therefore he would solve his own problem, and attempt to create his own reality, as though God was far away or non-essential.

> But the illusion of godlessness soon evaporates at
> the coming of the Lord and with the sounding of
> His voice. However unready, we are summonsed
> to Him in the day of Judgment. [8]

Though the first couple sought to hide from God, in mercy, God sought them out.

God could have justly damned the man and the woman for their transgression. They had broken faith. They had rebelled against Him who had made them and ordained for them such a lofty calling.

But the LORD instead called out to them in love.

"Adam where are you?"

The Most High God knew where Adam was. He who knows all things, needs no information. When God asks a question it is to bring us to a realization of our estrangement and to a humble confession of sin.

By His searching questions perhaps we can be brought to the place where we realize where our sins have brought us, and to look up to Him alone who can save us.

In this tender act, He showed us that His intention for man is salvation, and not solely justice. Even in the wording of the question there was no scathing reproach of Adam. It was a fatherly question, as though He were asking, *"Where are you son? Have you found what you were looking for in sin?"*

In calling out to Adam, God was requiring of him some introspection, some consideration of his actions, and acknowledgement of the breach that it might be healed.

In the New Testament hiding from God is called "remaining in darkness". It is the effort to not be known of God, the attempted refusal to be seen as we truly are, the resistance to an honest facing-up to our actions in the sight of God.

Christian conversion is called "walking in the light". It is nothing less than the willingness to be known by God, the acceptance of God's evaluation of our state, the open confession of sin and unrighteousness.

Jesus would characterize everyone in the world, as being either those who love the light and come to it, or those who love the darkness because their deeds are evil. This evaluation is the very basis for final judgment.

> And this is the condemnation, that light is come into the world, and men loved darkness rather than light, because their deeds were evil. For every one that doeth evil hateth the light, neither cometh to the light, lest his deeds should be reproved. But he that doeth truth cometh to the light, that his deeds may be made manifest, that they are wrought in God (John 3:19-21).

<> <> <>

And he said, Who told thee that thou wast naked? Hast thou eaten of the tree, whereof I commanded thee that thou shouldest not eat? And the man

> said, The woman whom thou gavest to be with
> me, she gave me of the tree, and I did eat. And the
> LORD God said unto the woman, What is this that
> thou hast done? And the woman said, The serpent
> beguiled me, and I did eat. And the LORD God said
> unto the serpent, Because thou hast done this, thou
> art cursed above all cattle, and above every beast of
> the field; upon thy belly shalt thou go, and dust shalt
> thou eat all the days of thy life (Genesis 3:11-14).

MEN DON'T SEEK AFTER God; they run from Him, as Adam did. The various false religions have not come about because man was seeking God with all of his heart, but in some misguided way. The sons of Adam are not misguided, but rebellious. They hate God, and seek to manufacture their own substitute gods in His place. False religion is a monument to the refusal of man to turn to the "only true God, and Jesus Christ whom He has sent".

Paul tells us that men are under divine wrath, not because of their ignorance of truth, but rather their evasion of it. Men stubbornly refuse to acknowledge, or to give due worship to the Creator.

> For the wrath of God is revealed from heaven against
> all ungodliness and unrighteousness of men, who
> hold the truth in unrighteousness; Because that
> which may be known of God is manifest in them;
> for God hath shewed it unto them (Romans 1:18-
> 19).

God asked Adam two direct questions. "Who told you that you were naked?" And, "Have you eaten of the tree, which I commanded you not to eat?"

The first question was designed to get Adam to look beyond the consequences of the sin (nakedness), and to admit the sin itself. Sinners readily bemoan the consequences of their sins, but are loathe to consider how they came to be.

The second question is more direct. Note the way it is worded—"the tree that **I commanded you** not to eat?" In other words, "Admit it Adam. Did you disobey Me? Yes or No?"

Fellowship, which is broken, is impossible to restore without a confession. If there is to be any repair of the breach, the offender must admit his transgression in as frank a way as possible.

King David showed us the way, when, after months of hypocrisy, depression, and soul sickness caused by the refusal to confess his sin, he was brought to the point where he poured out of an anguished heart,

> **Against you only have I sinned and done this evil in thy sight . . .**

But sin had made Adam devious, complicated and cowardly. He couldn't just admit his sin, even when God gave him a straightforward opportunity to know by experience, *"Whosoever confesses and forsakes his sins shall find mercy"*.

Adam had to preface his answer to God's question, with a self-serving excuse. He first blamed Eve and God, *"The woman **You gave me** . . . she gave me of the tree"*, then admitted "I did eat" of the tree.

Since Adam wouldn't simply admit his sin, there wasn't, at that point, much more to say to him, so God turned to Eve, his helpmeet.

"What is it that you have done?" This was a very simple question, which was also a call for humble and forthright confession. But like her husband, Eve also hid from God's searching light, blaming in this case, the serpent. *"The serpent beguiled me and I did eat"*.

It is true that Eve was indeed deceived by the serpent,

not Adam. Paul refered to this fact when he made the case that leadership and teaching in the church of God should be primarily male, based upon the vulnerability of women to spiritual seduction.

> But I suffer not a woman to teach, nor to usurp authority over the man, but to be in silence. For Adam was first formed, then Eve. And Adam was not deceived, but the woman being deceived was in the transgression (1 Timothy 2:12-14).

In no way was this a condemnation of Eve over Adam. In fact this shows that Adam's sin was far worse than Eve's. She could truly say that she was deceived; Adam was a blatant transgressor, a rebel against God.

The LORD then turned to the serpent but note that the tone was entirely different here. There was no gentle urging to confess, no call for introspection, for there was no divine intention to save the intelligent, moral being who spoke through the serpent.

All of the animal kingdom came under a curse because of Adam's sin. But the serpent would bear a particularly humiliating curse, for he allowed himself to be used by the evil one. Therefore he would have to crawl on the dust and feed on uncleanness, as a sign of the ultimate judgment coming upon the one to whom the serpent yielded.

<> <> <>

The Ray of Hope

> And I will put enmity between thee and the woman, and between thy seed and her seed; it shall bruise thy head, and thou shalt bruise his heel (Genesis 3:15).

THE BIBLE BEGINS WITH a woman and a serpent, but in Revelation 12 the vision at the end is of another woman, and by now the serpent has become a dragon, whose end is to be "cast down".

> And the great dragon was cast out, that old serpent, called the Devil, and Satan, which deceiveth the whole world: he was cast out into the earth, and his angels were cast out with him (Revelation 12:9).

Who is the serpent/dragon? The "old serpent" is none other than the devil (literally "accuser"), Satan (literally "enemy"), the former archangel named Lucifer. This is the one to whom the "seed of the woman" prophecy was directly addressed.

This prophecy occurred in the garden, at the meeting place of human failure and divine wrath, where the sinners stood before the Judge listening, trembling and awaiting sentencing.

It was in that very judgment pronounced upon the serpent, that a ray of hope and grace streamed through the gloom toward the guilty couple.

For Adam and Eve overheard that there would come through the woman a Seed who would one day deal a capital blow to the serpent, and by implication undo all the damage he had wrought.

Paul would one day tell us by the Holy Spirit, that "where sin abounds, grace does much more abound". Thus, any damage done to the human race by the sin of Adam, would be more than countered by a greater Adam, yea, even the last Adam, Jesus Christ.

And in this prophecy God established from the beginning, the rough outline of all of human history. Yet, in it He assured us of the ultimate outcome—the triumph of the

Seed of the woman over the serpent.

We would do well to take a little time to unpack this potent word.

First of all however, it is significant to note that the answer is said to come through the woman, and not through Adam. The serpent indeed deceived the woman, however the LORD never makes her responsible for the Fall. Remember that Adam was there with her when she took the fruit.

He was the one who was given the commission by God. He was the one who had received the word directly from God. He stood there listening to that word misrepresented and twisted and did nothing about it! To Adam was vouchsafed the entire human race. When he fell, we fell, for all of us were "in Adam" and not "in Eve".

Thus Adam's sin has vastly greater consequences.

Through the woman would come a Seed, who would undo the damage. In childbearing the human race shall be saved, for a child will come, through the woman who would be able to reverse the curse! Hallelujah!

<> <> <>

And I will put enmity between thee and the woman, and between thy seed and her seed; it shall bruise thy head, and thou shalt bruise his heel (Genesis 3:15).

THE GLOOM OF JUDGMENT and wrath at the sinners in the garden has been penetrated by this mysterious pronouncement of God, addressed to the serpent, and not to the guilty man and woman who had already refused accountability to God. Adam and Eve overhear, in the sentence passed upon the serpent, the possibility of a reversal.

Evidently even in judgment, the Lord remembers mercy to the fallen couple, for the woman shall bear a Son who will ultimately crush the serpent's head.

This *"proto evangel"*, (first gospel) came accompanied with the dark outline of the entire development of the human race even up to today. It is instructive to look at this brief but potent word of God.

I will put enmity between thee and the woman

FIRST OF ALL, GOD says that He Himself will be the instigator of this inveterate enmity, which will pulse through all future ages until the time of the final blow to the serpent.

The human race is to be polarized; there will be an invisible divide which will run through the heart of every man. Neutrality will be impossible, and any compromise or accommodation will prove to aid the cause of the serpent, not of the woman.

Jesus, the Son of God will one day echo this word when He will proclaim:

> Think not that I am come to send peace on earth:
> I came not to send peace, but a sword. For I
> am come to set a man at variance against his
> father, and the daughter against her mother, and
> the daughter in law against her mother in law
> (Matthew 10:34-35).

And the apostle John also warns us of this very enmity, when he says,

> Behold, what manner of love the Father hath
> bestowed upon us, that we should be called the
> sons of God: therefore the world knoweth us not,
> because it knew him not . . . Marvel not that the
> world hates you bretheren (1 John 3:1.13).

Again Jesus, on the night that He was betrayed, warned the little company of His followers,

> If the world hate you, ye know that it hated me

before it hated you. If ye were of the world, the world would love his own: but because ye are not of the world, but I have chosen you out of the world, therefore the world hateth you. Remember the word that I said unto you, The servant is not greater than his lord. If they have persecuted me, they will also persecute you; if they have kept my saying, they will keep yours also (John 15:18-20).

Satan hates all mankind but has a special hatred for women . . . The devil hates women particularly, because the salvation of man would be born of a woman. This is why false religion such as Islam is so harsh and unjust to women, using and abusing them like so many chattels.

Secularism, also being satanic, is hateful of true woman-hood. What is feminism but the hatred of the truly female? It is war on motherhood, nurture, love and support of men, marriage, romance and loyalty. The greatest modern expression of the serpent's hatred of women would have to be abortion and its twisted twin, homosexuality. Ironically this generation imagines that it has exalted the status of women, when in truth it is ruthlessly destroying it.

But there is a typological understanding of "the woman". The Book of Proverbs is a revelation of God that revolves around the choice of a young prince, between two women; the gaudy harlot and/or the virtuous wife. Both women offer wisdom, and call out to the young and naive, but only one of the women is true and can lead to God. The other woman's steps lead to death and hell.

Revelation likewise features two metaphorical women—the appalling *"great whore . . . mystery Babylon"*, and *"the Bride, the Lamb's wife"*. In Scripture, women are metaphors for spiritualities. There is a true woman, whom the serpent hates; she encompasses the true congregation of God. She is called the daughter of Zion, the Bride of the Lamb, for there is an unbroken continuity from Old to New

Testaments.

The serpent hates the woman, and has always sought to defile or destroy her. This is the meaning of the hatred of Israel, the wayward wife of the LORD. This is also the reason why the true church has always been persecuted and rejected.

In the beginning of the Bible there is a talk between a woman, and a serpent in a garden, a fallen angel. She and her husband in effect said "yes" to the devil, and "no" to God.

At the time of the Incarnation of God, in the annunciation to Mary, we also have a conversation between a woman, and an unfallen angel, Gabriel. She said, "yes" to God, and so too, did her engaged husband-to-be.

And at the end of the Bible, in the Revelation we have a vision of a woman, clothed in the sun, crowned with twelve stars, writhing in agony of childbirth as a consequence of saying "yes" to God. She is confronted by a terrible dragon (this is how the serpent would develop), who hates her and her seed, seeking to destroy them.

But he can't, for she is God's woman.

> And I will put enmity between thee and the woman, and between thy seed and her seed; it shall bruise thy head, and thou shalt bruise his heel (Genesis 3:15).

In the midst of the judgment pronounced by the LORD upon the serpent, He utters a promise, concerning the course of human history and its eventual outcome. The "seed" of the woman would ever be in conflict with the "seed" of the serpent. The conflict would culminate in an individual "Seed of the woman" who would crush the head of the serpent, but would greatly suffer doing so.

There is both a corporate and an individual identity to the two seeds.

Neither the woman or the serpent (Satan) have physical seed, therefore this is not a physical designation. There is no physical race of men who could identify as the "seed of the woman", nor is there a naturally accursed race that is the "seed of the serpent". In truth, there is only one race, the human race.

In an individual sense, *"the seed of the woman"* is the Messiah of Israel, born of the virgin, and destined to destroy *"death and to bring light and immortality to light through the gospel"* of His vicarious suffering and victory on the cross!

The individual "seed of the serpent" is the one who comes to be known as the Anti-Christ, the "Son of Perdition", the man who *"opposes all that is called God or that is worshipped as God",* that he might deceive the whole world into worshipping the serpent in a final apostasy.

Corporately speaking, the prophecy is about the spiritual and moral affinity of the whole human race.

The seed of the serpent consists of all of those who abide in the same spirit of independent pride as Lucifer did when he asserted his own will and goals over those of the Most High. It encompasses all who stubbornly refuse to agree with God that they are sinners, lost and in need of God's forgiveness.

These are the ones who refuse to acknowledge God or thank Him, much less admit their own helpless condition, or the need to be saved by the God appointed substitute, Jesus Christ. Proudly, they deny the need for salvation.

The God-resisting "seed of the serpent" always take the side of the serpent in the issues of their own day, whether they actually believe in the devil or not.

Jesus rebuked Peter, saying he was like Satan because he *"savored the things which be of men and not of God".* Satan is a humanist, not a Satanist. He savors the things that "be of men", e.g., human autonomy, pride, independence from God.

The seed of the serpent constantly alternate between the denial of God's existence, or complaint about the concept of a "merciful God" in view of the perceived injustice of the world. They don't hesitate to defy God's revealed will, for they allow themselves no reverence for Him.

They actually believe the serpent's lie, considering themselves, or man in general to be "as gods", able to define for himself right and wrong, good or evil, beauty and meaning, with no reference to the real God.

These are the God-resisting "brood of vipers" that John the Baptist railed against, the children of their (true) father, the devil, and who never fail to take the stand of their father, against the Most High.

> But when he saw many of the Pharisees and Sadducees come to his baptism, he said unto them, O generation of vipers, who hath warned you to flee from the wrath to come? Bring forth therefore fruits meet for repentance (Matthew 3:7-8).

> O generation of vipers, how can ye, being evil, speak good things? for out of the abundance of the heart the mouth speaketh (Matthew 12:34).

> Ye are of your father the devil, and the lusts of your father ye will do. He was a murderer from the beginning, and abode not in the truth, because there is no truth in him. When he speaketh a lie, he speaketh of his own: for he is a liar, and the father of it. And because I tell you the truth, ye believe me not (John 8:44-45).

Nimrod, Caesar Nero, Hitler, Stalin, and in fact all deified kings and leaders serve as types and shadows of the final *"seed of the serpent"*, the very *"son of perdition"* set to oppose all that is called God or that is worshipped as God, until the Lord comes to *"destroy him with the spirit of his mouth and with the brightness of his coming . . ."*.

> Let no man deceive you by any means: for that day shall not come, except there come a falling away first, and that man of sin be revealed, the son of perdition; Who opposeth and exalteth himself above all that is called God, or that is worshipped; so that he as God sitteth in the temple of God, shewing himself that he is God (2 Thessalonians 2:3-4).

> And then shall that Wicked be revealed, whom the Lord shall consume with the spirit of his mouth, and shall destroy with the brightness of his coming (2 Thessalonians 2:8).

Who are the seed of the woman? They consist of all of those down through time who stand with Adam and Eve on the ground of the first promise of salvation, and who patiently wait for the Lord to descend from heaven to save them and to undo the work of the serpent. They admit that they are helpless sinners in need of a God-sent savior. They are those who humbly acknowledge that sin requires death, and yet they rely on the God-appointed substitute. The seed of the woman are all pilgrims who will have to endure persecution in view of the eternal prize, all the while expecting the final triumph of the Redeemer.

The ultimate individual "Seed of the woman" is Jesus Christ, the one born of the virgin, or as Galatians 4 says, "born of a woman". He it is who has already "crushed the serpent's head" when He died on Calvary, and made a way for the fallen sons and daughters of Adam to be reconciled to God and born again.

> And I will put enmity between thee and the
> woman, and between thy seed and her seed; it
> shall bruise thy head, and thou shalt bruise his
> heel (Genesis 3:15).

The promise in Genesis looks past the fall of Adam and Eve, and even past the ongoing conflict between the two seeds, unto Calvary, where Jesus gained the triumph over the serpent. Ultimately, it also includes events beyond Calvary, to the *Parousia* of Jesus, and the crushing of the antichrist's head and the worldwide revolt that he leads. This mysterious vision even encompasses the final and irreversible crushing of the serpent's head when . . .

> And the devil that deceived them was cast into the
> lake of fire and brimstone, where the beast and
> the false prophet are, and shall be tormented day
> and night for ever and ever (Revelation 20:10).

The prophesied crushing of the serpent's head has been anticipated by the prophets and in various episodes of salvation history. Consider the strange story of Balaam.

When the children of Israel made their exodus out of Egypt, the nations trembled in fear. A Midianite king named Balak ruled Moab. He hired a pagan prophet named Balaam from what is now known as Iraq, to curse Israel so that they would not be able to repossess their land.

When Balaam presented himself to the king, he warned him that he could only say what the LORD told him to, having been warned by God already. Every time he attempted to curse Israel, amazing blessings came out of his mouth, for he prophesied the separation, fruitfulness and prowess of Israel, from three different locations around their camp!

Finally the enraged Arabian king ordered the prophet to go home. But the Spirit of God wasn't done.

> And now, behold, I go unto my people: come therefore, and I will advertise thee what this people shall do to thy people in the latter days . . . I shall see him, but not now: I shall behold him, but not nigh: there shall come a Star out of Jacob, and a Sceptre shall rise out of Israel, and shall smite the corners of Moab, and destroy all the children of Sheth (Numbers 24:14-17).

In the last days, a star shall arise from Jacob, a Scepter from Israel, who (literally) "shall smite the head of Moab" and "destroy the children (literally) of Tumult". The head blow to Moab, (as the representative of all of heathendom) typifies the victory of the seed of the woman.

The story of Deborah also comes to mind. When God routed the numerically and technologically superior army of the Canaanites, the pagan general Sisera fled the battlefield on foot, eventually seeking refuge in the tent of the wife of a perceived ally.

But Jael was a believer in the God of Israel. She gave the exhausted general warm milk, and allowed him to rest his weary head in her tent. When he fell asleep, she pulled out a tent stake and a hammer and drove the stake into his temple! For this the Spirit of God called her "blessed above women", the same blessing Gabrielle would pronounce upon Mary.

> **Blessed above women** shall Jael the wife of Heber the Kenite be, blessed shall she be above women in the tent. He asked water, and she gave him milk; she brought forth butter in a lordly dish. She put her hand to the nail, and her right hand to the workmen's hammer; and with the hammer she smote Sisera, she smote off his head, when she had pierced and stricken through his temples. At her feet he bowed, he fell, he lay down: at her feet he bowed, he fell: where he bowed, there he fell down dead (Judges 5:24-27).

There is a story in 1 Samuel, which also portends the crushing of the serpent's head. I refer to the capture of the Ark in the battle of Aphek, (1 Samuel 4-6). The gospel is portrayed there, for the Ark being a type of Jesus, was "handed over to the Gentiles" by the corrupt Jewish high priests. What looked to be a catastrophic defeat, "Ichabod", was turned instead to a great demonstration to the pagans of Jahweh's superiority.

When the Philistines put the Ark in the temple of Dagon, (a tomb of death and decay) they thought Dagon had triumphed. But when they rose early the next morning to resume their celebration of the death of the God of Israel, they found out He wasn't as dead as they imagined Him to be, for they found Dagon prostrated before him.

So they propped their god back up again, in his own temple. But when they came back the next morning, this time Dagon's head and hands were broken! He shall bruise the serpent's head!

Perhaps the greatest type of the victory of the seed of the woman over the serpent is seen in the story of David and Goliath.

Goliath was the champion of his people, the representative of heathendom, taunting and abusing the faith of the people of God. Note that he is described as covered in a "coat of mail", like a scaly serpent. Like the coming Antichrist, the serpent stood there openly defying God and the people of God.

There are sixes all over the description of Goliath, for he was six cubits tall, had six pieces of armor and the head of his spear weighed six hundred shekels!

But David (from Bethlehem) slung a stone, which crushed Goliath's head! Thus was the ultimate triumph anticipated—the seed of the woman shall indeed confront the serpent and deal a deadly head wound.

> And David put his hand in his bag, and took thence
> a stone, and slang it, and smote the Philistine in
> his forehead, that the stone sunk into his fore-
> head; and he fell upon his face to the earth. So
> David prevailed over the Philistine with a sling
> and with a stone, and smote the Philistine, and
> slew him; but there was no sword in the hand of
> David. Therefore David ran, and stood upon the
> Philistine, and took his sword, and drew it out of
> the sheath thereof, and slew him, and cut off his
> head therewith. And when the Philistines saw
> their champion was dead, they fled (1 Samuel
> 17:49-51).

Finally the Book of Revelation features an enemy of God who has a "deadly head wound" that has been healed. The whole world will end up worshipping this "beast", whose end will be the lake of fire.

> And I saw one of his heads as it were wounded
> to death; and his deadly wound was healed: and
> all the world wondered after the beast. And they
> worshipped the dragon which gave power unto
> the beast: and they worshipped the beast, saying,
> Who is like unto the beast? who is able to make
> war with him? (Revelation 13:3-4).

The crushing of the serpent's head in one sense has al-ready occurred, in the victory of the Son of God on the cross of Calvary. Satan's work has been destroyed. Man has been reconciled to God. The doom of this world is assured for the final sentence has been passed. Jesus announced on His way to Jerusalem to His death,

> Now is the judgment of this world: now shall the
> prince of this world be cast out. And I, if I be lifted
> up from the earth, will draw all men unto me
> (John 12:31-32).

But there is another sense in which the rebellion of man is going to be allowed to come to a final head. Satan's man will emerge; the antichrist will arise to unite the seed of the serpent in their final opposition to God, for *"the Kings of the earth and their rulers have taken counsel together against the Lord and His Christ".*

The "head" of the serpent will be crushed again when the Lord comes back as a *"stone not made with human hands",* and shatters the proud statue of man erected in honor of the serpent's lie that man can be "as gods". *The kingdoms of this world will then become the kingdoms of our Lord and of His Christ!*

The serpent's end will be when he is thrown into the lake of fire, with all of those who sided with him. That will be the final crushing of the serpent's head by the seed of the woman! Hallelujah!

5

Consequences

Unto the woman he said, I will greatly multiply thy sorrow and thy conception; in sorrow thou shalt bring forth children; and thy desire shall be to thy husband, and he shall rule over thee. And unto Adam he said, Because thou hast hearkened unto the voice of thy wife, and hast eaten of the tree, of which I commanded thee, saying, Thou shalt not eat of it: cursed is the ground for thy sake; in sorrow shalt thou eat of it all the days of thy life; Thorns also and thistles shall it bring forth to thee; and thou shalt eat the herb of the field; In the sweat of thy face shalt thou eat bread, till thou return unto the ground; for out of it wast thou taken: for dust thou art, and unto dust shalt thou return (Genesis 3:16-19).

IT WAS ONLY AFTER the announcement of the gospel of the "seed of the woman", that the temporal sentence was passed upon the transgressors. To the man and the woman, each in their respective God-assigned spheres of life, came care, sorrow, and frustrating toil.

To the woman who listened to the serpent, sorrow was

multiplied in the area of conception, birth, and marriage. The problem included but went far beyond the uniquely feminine ordeals of ovulation and pain in childbirth.

God said that He would "greatly multiply" the sorrow, conception and childbirth! Did Adam and Eve realize that they would be the parents of billions of children? Though every birth of a baby is a joy, always it is mingled with sorrow, because each child soon evidences the original sin of Adam, and is thus a reminder of our first parent's sin.

> Behold, I was shapen in iniquity; and in sin did my mother conceive me (Psalm 51:5).

This is why childbirth itself required special offerings and cleansings in the Law of God. Babies are born sinners; the sin of the garden is constantly multiplied. Circumcision also teaches this, because it presupposes guilt. Children are not born righteous. They are not all right "just as they are". They are little Adams and Eves with corrupted natures, passed down through birth.

Conception is cause for sorrow mingled with joy in a fallen world, estranged and alienated from God. Children are indeed a blessing, and to conceive a child is a privilege given to us of love. But what shall become of that precious child? How will his/her life develop? How many mothers have cried bitter tears for a child gone astray?

In the best of marriages and circumstances, we can catch but a glimpse of the astonishing beauty of the original plan. The joy of man and wife bringing children into God's world, rearing them together in love, security and order, that they might mature and repeat the blessed cycle. *"Be fruitful and multiply and subdue the earth"*, the original vision, or as the Psalms put it—

> Blessed is every one that feareth the LORD; that

walketh in his ways. For thou shalt eat the labour of thine hands: happy shalt thou be, and it shall be well with thee.Thy wife shall be as a fruitful vine by the sides of thine house: thy children like olive plants round about thy table.Behold, that thus shall the man be blessed that feareth the LORD. The LORD shall bless thee out of Zion: and thou shalt see the good of Jerusalem all the days of thy life. Yea, thou shalt see thy children's children, and peace upon Israel (Psalm 128).

But in the world now run by the fallen sons of Adam and Eve, conception often occurs out of marriage, without love, and as an evidence of shame. The USA alone recently passed the abominable landmark of its fifty-millionth abortion. How awful! Woe to us! God says in Proverbs 8 that all those who *"hate Me love death!"*.

Another aspect of the sentence upon the woman was that the delicate balance between man and woman would now be skewed, and the woman would suffer greatly because of it, particularly in marriage.

"Your desire will be to your husband . . ." was not a blessing although it sounds innocent enough. What was being said was that she would be vulnerable and in a position of utter dependence upon him. In a sinful world she will need him more than he will "need" her.

It has been pointed out that this is similar to a phrase in Genesis 4 where God warns Cain that sin desires to rule him. If so, this is saying that insecurity within the woman will cause her to seek to rule in the marriage over her husband.

In fact though, *he shall rule over you . . .* in this sinful, fallen world. The man has ruled by his strength and by the perversion of his position as the "head". Most of human history has alternated between deifying women, or harshly suppressing them, both of which are hurtful to women.

No woman can live up to the perfection of an Aphrodite, or an Athena, or a Madonna. Idealizing women actually debases and suppresses them, as our modern pornographic culture demonstrates.

One need only look as far as the Muslim world to see the satanic hatred of women lived out among the one billion adherents of the cult formed around a pirate, rapist and murderer.

The Law of Moses was a definite elevation of the status of women, but it was only the morning star compared to the Sunrise of the coming of Jesus Christ into this world as far as the restoration of the respect originally intended for women by the Creator.

But in this age of darkness and declension from the Revelation of Jesus Christ, women are once again coming under the full brunt of this curse. Every so-called modern liberation movement celebrated in the West as emancipatory, has actually destroyed the status of women.

Feminism is actually hateful to true womanhood. The liberation from marriage has helped the "playboys" of the world but consigned millions of women to single parenthood, and poverty. "No fault" divorce laws lobbied for by feminists have worked in favor of immoral men, but hurt women.

Pornography debases women. The so-called "sexual revolution" has made for women, a coarser, ruder, harsher world, than the Judeo-Christian world, which it supplanted. Love and romance are virtually dead in our brave new (godless) world.

Finally though, with joy we realize that this curse is temporal, for soon the "seed of the woman" returns to bring in a better order. Maranatha!

<> <> <>

*And unto Adam he said, Because thou hast
hearkened unto the voice of thy wife, and hast eaten
of the tree, of which I commanded thee, saying,
Thou shalt not eat of it: cursed is the ground for
thy sake; in sorrow shalt thou eat of it all the days
of thy life; Thorns also and thistles shall it bring
forth to thee; and thou shalt eat the herb of the
field; In the sweat of thy face shalt thou eat bread,
till thou return unto the ground; for out of it wast
thou taken: for dust thou art, and unto dust shalt
thou return (Genesis 3: 17-19).*

ADAM HAD EARLIER PLEADED before the Judge that he ate of
the tree because *"the woman, you gave me ... gave me of the
tree and I did eat"*, as if that would be a mitigating factor in
his crime. But in the sentence upon Adam, the LORD cited
the fact that Adam listened to her and not to God as an ag-
gravation of his transgression.

"Because you hearkened unto the voice of your wife ..."
all these terrible things will come to pass.

Note also how the LORD words it, *"You did eat of the tree
which I commanded thee not to eat ..."*, framing Adam's sin
as a blatant transgression, and as an affront to the authority
of God Himself. Adam was not deceived; he simply defied
the Word of God. Adam was a rebel.

Therefore into all of the areas, which pertained to Adam
specifically, came sorrow, care, and frustrating futility.

The ground, which was originally designed to yield to
his cultivation, bringing forth its abundance, would now re-
sist his efforts. Thorns and thistles are an apt representa-
tion of the ever-multiplying, relentless and fruitless compli-
cations man would now labor under to coax a living under
the now hostile soil.

Animals became apprehensive, fearful and even hostile.

Flowers began to fade, and fruit rotted on the vine, as it became painfully obvious that the earth could no longer be home. The age of decay and death commenced as a result of Adam's sin.

The Epistle to the Romans tells us that it was God Himself who subjected the creation to vanity, and that He did it in hope. The bondage to decay, as Romans also calls it, was imposed upon the creation so that man would not be able to try to build a life here without God. God wants man to turn to him and to be fitted for the New Creation.

> For the earnest expectation of the creature waiteth for the manifestation of the sons of God. For the creature was made subject to vanity, not willingly, but by reason of him who hath subjected the same in hope, Because the creature itself also shall be delivered from the bondage of corruption into the glorious liberty of the children of God (Romans 8:19-21).

Ecclesiastes also reveals that divine judgment was the cause of the curse of vanity in this world. The preacher expounds upon the "the crookedness that cannot be made straight" in this life, which prevents fallen man from being able to create a lasting, satisfactory civilization. Ever since the Fall there is something perverse about man. We are crooked and conflicted, for we have "eternity in our hearts" but are natural and subject to death. This is the "burden of God".

Adam's sin had a far greater impact than Eve's for by his sin we were estranged from our very environment, as well as from our God. Adam's sin was so impacting it caused the whole of Adam's race to become transgressors. His sin corrupted our very nature, for the whole of the human race was said to be "in Adam".

> Therefore as by the offence of one judgment came upon all men to condemnation; even so by the righteousness of one the free gift came upon all men unto justification of life. For as **by one man's disobedience many were made sinners**, so by the obedience of one shall many be made righteous (Romans 5:18-19).

The final pronouncement of the consequence of Adam's was the grim sentence of physical death. Adam would toil in the cursed fields, living by the very "sweat of his brow" until . . .

Until what? *Until you return to the ground.* We work until we die. That's it? What a bitter letdown for the man who began with such regal potential! He was made to be regent, lord of the earth. He was the acme of creation and walked and worked with the Most High God, only to end as an empty shell? Lowered into the dirt to rot?

This was the sentence given by the Judge to the transgressor; spoken in a play on words. *"For dust* (Adam) *you are and unto dust* (Adamah) *you shall return".*

For this reason the sons of Adam have never been able to accept death as natural. Death is deeply feared because of the innate knowledge that it is a penalty from God, and that it really isn't the end of man who was made in God's image.

Man's separation was complete--from His God, his wife, his environment, from his people, his work, and finally the separation of his own being, from body and soul. **The wages of sin is death** . . . but death is not the last word of Genesis 3. Skip ahead four verses. The last word of this chapter is *life*!

<> <> <>

And Adam called his wife's name Eve; because she was the mother of all living (Genesis 3:20).

EVERY DETAIL OF THIS foundational chapter is set in place by the Holy Spirit of God that we might benefit by this unique revelation of why the world is as it is.

Therefore the naming of Eve, who up to this point is referred to as *"Ishah", (the woman),* is not incidental, but of signal importance to we who believe.

The significance of the naming of Eve, (literally, "Chavah"), can only be appreciated when the dreadful sentence of death was passed upon Adam in the previous verse. "Adam (dust) you are and to Adamah (dirt) you shall return!"

Of all of the penalties pronounced upon Adam this one must have been the most awful and unthinkable. The man who had been created as God's regent, commissioned to "subdue the earth", and to "fill it" with his children, was sentenced to death, something he had no immediate understanding of.

Adam began dying from the time of the divine pronouncement. Death is separation, from God, from Eve, from love, well-being and shalom; it is depression, despair, breakdown, decay, disintegration, fear, illness, and finally at the end, a humiliating return to dust.

Because Adam and Eve revolted against their Creator, they had to die. Thus they were separated from their environment and from each other as well as from their God, who was the source of their life. Everything for them changed and those changes rapidly began to manifest themselves, as we will see.

They had to leave Eden, the garden of delight, the only home they have ever known, for they had forfeited it. They began to experience new emotions, such as shame, fear, remorse, and even deep regret. The couple must now endure the reign of death.

This is the context that is set for the naming of Eve, the

mother of all living. There are two interpretations for Adam's act of naming her. Either it was an act of proud defiance or of humble faith. The sons of Adam and Eve have alternated between the two options ever since.

If it was an act of defiance, Adam was saying, "We will live in spite of your sentence. We will make a life for ourselves. We will define life on our own terms. The children of Eve will indeed live!" Some speculate that the goddess worship of the ancients was actually "Eve" worship.

Goddess worship often involves serpent worship as well, and the pursuit of "hidden wisdom" runs throughout the universal paganistic mystery religion. The secret knowledge Eve was looking for is still sought by the fallen sons and daughters of Eve.

On the other hand, I believe that the naming of Eve was an act of faith. True, God had pronounced death upon the guilty couple, and in doing so, upon the whole race of men, but not until after he had indirectly given them the promise of life, that of the head crushing "seed of the woman" promised to come through the woman.

In view of that promise, Eve indeed became the "mother of all living", for in the birth of the promised seed, she shall indeed bring life! With the crushing of the serpent's head, comes the reversal of all that the serpent has wrought. The curse will be lifted and a new day will dawn for the sons of Adam.

Thus for Adam and Eve, through faith in the promise, the last word shall not be death and decay. Life shall again prevail.

They did indeed both die and were returned to the dust from which they came. But in continuity with all of the seed of the woman down through the generations, they looked forward to the day that prophets and apostles such as Isaiah and Paul, confidently proclaimed:

Your dead shall live; Together with my dead body they shall arise. Awake and sing, you who dwell in dust; For your dew is like the dew of herbs, And the earth shall cast out the dead (Isaiah 26:19).

Wherefore he saith, Awake thou that sleepest, and arise from the dead, and Christ shall give thee light (Ephesians 5:14).

<> <> <>

Unto Adam also and to his wife did the LORD God make coats of skins, and clothed them (Genesis 3:21).

REMEMBER THAT WHEN ADAM and Eve sinned they immediately perceived that they were naked? The nakedness of our first father and mother was a spiritual condition as well as a physical one. Now that they had broken away from God, they deeply sensed that they were vulnerable, uncovered, and exposed as sinful beings in the presence of holiness.

This sense of nakedness has passed down unto all of the children of Adam. All of us feel the need for some kind of covering of our innate shame. Even unbelievers in God have a psychological need for some sense of justification of their own lives, often seeking it in "do-goodism".

Adam and Eve constructed clothing of fig leaves in their vain attempt to deal with the sense of shame, caused by the Fall. None of us want to have to appear naked before the Holy God therefore we seek a covering.

But the fig leaves proved to be inadequate. They didn't truly remove the shame, for Adam and Eve fled from God, even though they were clothed in fig leaves. On the Judgment Day, all of man's accumulated "fig leaves" will prove to be insufficient as a covering for our shame.

The problems with fig leaves are manifold. First of all, they are the solution initiated and enacted by man. It was Adam's idea, his own solution to the profound spiritual, moral and psychological problem of nakedness, i.e., shame.

The fact that Adam's solution to the outcome of sin was rejected by God, is an early testament to what Paul the Apostle would make so clear, in Romans 3—

> Therefore by the deeds of the law there shall no flesh be justified in his sight: for by the law is the knowledge of sin (Romans 3:20).

We cannot be saved by good works, (fig leaves), for God doesn't accept them as satisfaction of His broken law. The solution can't come from fallen man; the best that man can do to justify himself. In the sight of God, thid is as abominable as filthy rags.

> But we are all as an unclean thing, and all our righteousnesses are as filthy rags; and we all do fade as a leaf; and our iniquities, like the wind, have taken us away (Isaiah 64:6).

Secondly, Adam's solution to the shame problem didn't address the real problem. In trying to cover over with fig leaves the sense of shame for what he had done, he showed a failure to appreciate the true nature of his sin, as well as the impact of it upon his God. He was trying to remedy guilt feelings, but not true moral guilt.

We men don't merely feel guilty; we are guilty. We have broken God's law, and by our self-will, we have disrupted God's universe. All of our sins are against God Himself. If there was to be a solution to the estrangement they have wrought, it had to come from God.

All of the false religious systems of the world, developed by the sons and daughters of Adam and Eve are man-centered. They are designed to recover the lost sense of covering, the "rightness" with God that Adam once took for granted and that even fallen men acutely sense.

They are mere fig leaves, man-centered works systems which prove wholly insensitive to the true claims of God and to the deepest need of man, which is not the eradication of guilty feelings, but the expiation of true and deep guilt.

This was the significance of the animal skin coverings. The fig leaves had to be removed; Adam and Eve had to forswear their own solution to the shame problem, in order to accept God's solution, which was the animal coverings.

On a practical level, it must have horrified them to see the dead lambs, rams or bulls that God skinned as He made them coverings. They had never seen physical death, the shedding of blood, or the tanning of hides. This was God's solution? It seemed so harsh, so barbaric, and so bloody!

Surely fig leaves were a more compassionate way of clothing oneself!

But the bloody skins were God's way, not the fig leaves, and like every other detail in this hugely significant chapter, they are of vast theological import. What was God teaching by this act of clothing them?

Substitution. The wages of sin is death. Therefore someone must die for sin, either the sinner or an innocent substitute. God's way of dealing with the shame of sin, is by the substitution of life for life.

It would later emerge in the unfolding of God's revelation that God knew we would sin and fall and need such a covering, and had already provided Jesus as *the Lamb of God slain from the foundation of the world*.

> And they sung a new song, saying, Thou art worthy to take the book, and to open the seals thereof:

for thou wast slain, and hast redeemed us to God by thy blood out of every kindred, and tongue, and people, and nation (Revelation 5:9).

But for the first couple, the testimony was the promise of the "seed of the woman" and the freshly slain animals, whose deaths provided an adequate covering. The first lesson God taught the newly fallen couple was the lesson that to them, worship would only be possible by way of blood sacrifice.

This they would pass on to their sons, one of whom would virulently reject the revelation, the other one would die as a martyr to it.

<> <> <>

And the LORD God said, Behold, the man is become as one of us, to know good and evil: and now, lest he put forth his hand, and take also of the tree of life, and eat, and live for ever: Therefore the LORD God sent him forth from the garden of Eden, to till the ground from whence he was taken. So he drove out the man; and he placed at the east of the garden of Eden Cherubims, and a flaming sword which turned every way, to keep the way of the tree of life (Genesis 3:22-24).

Oh, once we were happy, way back in the garden, but a lie broke the stillness, and our hearts began to harden . . . Larry Norman, In Another Land

ADAM AND EVE WERE convicted and sentenced for their crime against God. They had broken faith with the One who had made them, and forfeited their privileged place in God's holy garden.

But in mercy, the guilty couple had also been given the gospel of deliverance through the "seed of the woman" and taught the importance of worship through the blood of an innocent substitute.

What now?

THEY MUST BE DRIVEN out of the garden. God forcibly evicted them. They would have to live in a hostile world, suffering the consequences of the false wisdom they had opted for. Adam and Eve must toil and sweat, raise fallen children, and see the constant out-working of their transgression, from generation to generation until death.

They had to go out of the garden, for should they now, in their fallen state, illegitimately eat of the "tree of Life", they would be locked into the fallen state forever. Their doom would be irrevocable. God's love was severe in putting them out of the only home they had ever known, but if He would save them He must do so.

But ever since then, the sons and daughters of Adam and Eve have sought to gain some kind of access back into the garden. Fallen man would smash through the gates, or create his own (godless) version of the garden. Pagans and humanists alike lust either for the good old days that once were, or the "golden age" that is just around the corner again, according to the rhetoric of the various political and religious messiahs.

The Second Psalm warns us that the world's masses are being prepared for the arrival of an ultimate false "messiah" to inaugurate the new (godless) Eden. This is why the "kings of the earth and their rulers" are busy eradicating every public trace possible of the West's Judeo-Christian past.

> Why do the heathen rage, and the people imagine a vain thing? The kings of the earth set themselves, and the rulers take counsel together, against the LORD, and against his anointed, saying, Let us

break their bands asunder, and cast away their
cords from us (Psalm 2:1-3).

The fact that God put a turning sword at the entrance
and deployed awesome living creatures, (the cherubim),
implies that if he could, fallen man may try violently to seize
the garden for himself. The fallen sons of Adam would crash
through the walls.

This lust for something of Eden (without repentance)
runs deep in men's hearts. Isn't that what our modern drug
craze is all about? The obsession with illicit sex? As our
troubled culture departs from God, many just want to feel
better no matter what the cost, just to grasp a few minutes
of Edenic bliss if possible.

Fallen man lusts for a respite from the sentence pronounced upon us by God in the Fall, but never by turning in
humble repentance to God.

On a larger scale, consider the spectacle of atheistic
Communism which sought by violence to create an earthly Eden, in the name of a promised utopia. As Stalin once
famously said about the massive slaughter, the artificial
famine of his own people, and the violent repression he in-
stituted,

> One death is always a tragedy, millions of deaths
> are a statistic.

As human history has shown from the French Revolution, through the various Marxist revolutions, up to our
own turbulent time, when fallen man wants to re-create
Eden (utopia), it always ends up looking a lot like hell. Even
if man could concoct a godless Eden he would only corrupt
it, for man's heart is not right.

The social and sexual revolution of the 1960s was in the
same vein, as this famous line from the song "Woodstock"
attests:

We are stardust, we are golden, and we have got to get ourselves back to the garden . . . Joni Mitchell

It was another naive attempt to cast off all of our traditional Judeo-Christian restraints in an attempt to liberate mankind, hoping to get back to the natural state. Unfortunately they ignored the truth that since the Fall, man's natural state isn't love, harmony and peace; it is violent, selfish and grasping.

God drove Adam and Eve out of the garden. There will never be a return to Eden. God's plan for man is not backward looking, but forward. No, we cannot ever recover "paradise lost", but as pilgrims we look forward to the arrival of the "city whose builder and maker is God".

By faith Abraham, when he was called to go out into a place which he should after receive for an inheritance, obeyed; and he went out, not knowing whither he went. By faith he sojourned in the land of promise, as in a strange country, dwelling in tabernacles with Isaac and Jacob, the heirs with him of the same promise: For he looked for a **city which hath foundations, whose builder and maker is God** (Hebrews 11:8-10).

These all died in faith, not having received the promises, but having seen them afar off, and were persuaded of them, and embraced them, and confessed that they were strangers and pilgrims on the earth. For they that say such things declare plainly that they seek a country. And truly, if they had been mindful of that country from whence they came out, they might have had opportunity to have returned. But now they desire a better country, that is, an heavenly: wherefore God is not ashamed to be called their God: for he hath prepared for them a city (Hebrews 11:14-16)

<> <> <>

So he drove out the man; and he placed at the east of the garden of Eden Cherubims, and a flaming sword which turned every way, to keep the way of the tree of life (Genesis 3:24).

WE COME TO THE final verse of this momentous chapter of the Bible. By now, the LORD has indicted the guilty couple, along with the serpent, and pronounced a judgment upon the serpent. Within that condemnation of the serpent, was a promise of salvation for the man, his wife and their descendants.

The man and his wife also received the divine sentence upon them. The Lord's pronouncement was given. Toil, frustration, futility and sorrow would be their lot, until death. Then Adam and Eve were stripped of the fig coverings that they had made for themselves. The Lord slew an animal as a substitute for the sinners, taking its fleece to make for them a covering.

Finally, they were evicted from the garden of delight. The transgressors were driven out by the LORD. They could no longer stay where God had originally placed them. They would now have to make themselves a home in the hostile, sin-cursed world.

But as one of our expositors has noted, God set cherubim at the east end of the garden to "keep the way to the tree of life". This too, like the earliest gospel of the seed of the woman, and the animal covering, and the name of Eve, was a hopeful development. God assures us by this act, that there is yet a way to the Tree of Life; all was not lost.

Cherubim were set by the Lord to guard the way to the tree of life. These terrible, holy creatures show up at other places in the Scripture; transporting the pavement on which the throne of God is set in Ezekiel's vision; sitting on either side of the very throne of God on the lid of the Ark of the Covenant; and ceaselessly worshipping God in John's vision in Revelation.

> Then I looked, and, behold, in the firmament that was above the head of the cherubims there appeared over them as it were a sapphire stone, as the appearance of the likeness of a throne. And he spake unto the man clothed with linen, and said, Go in between the wheels, even under the cherub, and fill thine hand with coals of fire from between the cherubims, and scatter them over the city. And he went in in my sight. Now the cherubims stood on the right side of the house, when the man went in; and the cloud filled the inner court. Then the glory of the LORD went up from the cherub, and stood over the threshold of the house; and the house was filled with the cloud, and the court was full of the brightness of the LORD's glory. And the sound of the cherubims' wings was heard even to the outer court, as the voice of the Almighty God when he speaketh (Ezekiel 10:1-5).

Cherubim are evidently assigned to be guardians of God's glory, keeping away the sinners who would presume to enter heedlessly into the divine presence. God preserved the way to the tree of life, but no one would be able to access it among the unworthy sinners of the fallen race of Adam.

Thus the figures of the cherubim were woven into the very curtain, which separated The Holy Place from the outer court, and the Holy of Holies from the inner court.

> Make a curtain of blue, purple and scarlet yarn and finely twisted linen, with cherubim woven into it by a skilled worker (Exodus 26:31).

In Solomon's temple, not only were cherubim woven into curtains, and two golden ones sitting on the very lid of the mercy seat, but two fifteen foot cherubims of olive wood were carved, and overlaid with gold, and set in the holy place.

> And within the oracle he made two cherubims of olive tree, each ten cubits high (1 Kings 6:23).

The Holy Place of the tabernacle and temple are widely believed to be God-ordained models of the Garden of Eden. The Ark of God's presence in the Holy of Holies, served to represent the tree of life. The sanctuary, which was a model of the garden itself, featured the candelabra (tree of the knowledge of good and evil) shining upon the table of show bread, (Christ, the only truth), and the altar of incense for true worship.

But the cherubim on the holy curtain kept men away from the glory of God in the Holy of Holies. They reminded continually that none could draw near, for *"all have sinned and continually come short of the glory of God"*! The curtains were drawn. The cherubim on the curtains continually reinforced the separation. Sinful man was cut off. He could not draw near. the way to the tree of life was closed.

> Jesus, when he had cried again with a loud voice, yielded up the ghost. And, behold, the veil of the temple was rent in twain from the top to the bottom; and the earth did quake, and the rocks rent (Matthew 27:50-51).

What import this brings to the familiar detail of the crucifixion story, that when Jesus cried out with a loud voice, *"the veil in the temple was rent from top to bottom"*! Could it be? Has the way to the tree of life been now opened to us? Have the cherubim been enabled to step aside and let the believing sinner draw near to God?

> Having therefore, brethren, boldness to enter into the holiest by the blood of Jesus, By a new and living way, which he hath consecrated for us, through the veil, that is to say, his flesh; And having an high priest over the house of God; Let us draw near with a true heart in full assurance of faith, having our hearts sprinkled from an evil conscience, and our bodies washed with pure water (Hebrews 10:19-22).

The cherubim appear again in John's Revelation, for all things in Genesis have their resolution in Revelation. They appear in all of their holy awfulness, but this time not as an opposition to men, but in harmony with the redeemed sons of Adam, worshipping the LORD and the Lamb who by his own blood has purchased us.

> And when he had taken the book, the four beasts and four and twenty elders fell down before the Lamb, having every one of them harps, and golden vials full of odours, which are the prayers of saints. And they sung a new song, saying, Thou art worthy to take the book, and to open the seals thereof: for thou wast slain, and hast redeemed us to God by thy blood out of every kindred, and tongue, and people, and nation; And hast made us unto our God kings and priests: and we shall reign on the earth (Revelation 5:8-10).

As I said earlier, the last word of this solemn, grave chapter of the Bible is not death, but life. In spite of man's sin and failure, God's mercy triumphs. There is a way back to the tree of life. There is a "Seed of the woman" who has come. The blood of Jesus does indeed cleanse us from all sin! Hallelujah!

6

Cain and Abel: True and False Worship

*And Adam knew Eve his wife; and she conceived,
and bare Cain, and said, I have gotten a man from
the Lord. And she again bare his brother Abel. And
Abel was a keeper of sheep, but Cain was a tiller of
the ground (Genesis 4:1-2).*

BY NOW, ADAM AND Eve had been evicted from their home,
the garden of delight, because of their sin. They were not allowed to remain or to eat of the precious "Tree of Life". In fact
it would have been spiritually disastrous for them to do so.

They had rejected God's glory. They chose not to remain
within the limits God had set for them; neither did they
accept the Word of God which warned them of the consequences of transgressing the divine command.

Instead, the first couple chose to judge "good and evil"
for themselves. They tried the fruit because they actually believed the alternative "word", which was presented
to them in the garden, the word of the serpent, over and
against the Word of God.

Like so many millions of their descendents, the first
man and woman learned by bitter experience that the Word

of God was true after all. They had fallen, and they knew it immediately for fear filled their very being. They would have to be called into account by their Lord for what they had done!

The reality of judgment sent them into hiding. But no matter how ill prepared, they would be brought out into the light to give an answer.

The Lord came to them, and after a brief arraignment and trial, the serpent, the man and woman received their respective sentences. The man and the woman were banished from the garden of delights. She would conceive and bear children in sorrow, and become utterly dependent upon her husband. The man would be consigned to painful, frustrating toil. Thorns and thistles would hinder and vex his life's work, and at the end, the ultimate futility, death, dissolution and return to the earth from which he (and she) came! The serpent would be humiliated. He would crawl on his belly and feed on the dust until the time appointed for his final judgment.

But the gloom of the trial was penetrated by a gleaming shaft of light, for the Lord made a promise, indirectly to the man and woman, (for they had refused accountability). To the serpent the Lord pronounced these words of promise,

> And I will put enmity between thee and the woman, and between thy seed and her seed; it shall bruise thy head, and thou shalt bruise his heel (Genesis 3:15).

So, there would be a deliverer for the man and the woman! The woman who had been seduced by evil, lending her ear to the alternate "word" of God, and who with her husband had heeded the vicious accusation against the character of God, would now be the God-assigned vessel to bring forth a deliverer. What grace!

The coming "seed of the woman" would indeed crush the serpent's head, but the victory would be costly and painful, for the serpent would bruise the heel of the "seed of the woman".

As a token of the coming suffering of the "seed of the woman", which would procure the couple's deliverance, the LORD removed the homemade fig leaf covering that the newly self-conscious couple had manufactured, and clothed them with the skin of an animal which He had slaughtered. This was their first encounter with physical death, and it must have appalled them.

All that remained now for the exiled couple was to cling to the promise, as they sought to make a life for themselves in the now hostile world. They worked hard, learned to love each other, bore children and waited for the time when the woman would bear "the seed of the woman" who would come and undo the curse once and for all.

This is the setting for the first two verses of our text. God saw to it that even in judgment there would be mercy for the man and his wife. There were still comforts within the exile. Adam and Eve had each other. *Adam knew his wife* ... The two of them could uphold each other, and somewhat help to ease the tensions, fears and sorrows of their alienation.

They could still appeal to God from a distance, but only by offering the God-appointed sacrifices which served to underscore the divine teaching that sin deserved death, but also the hopeful message that God could be approached through a substitute.

When Eve conceived and bore son, it seemed that at long last the promise was in the process of fulfillment. They named him Cain, "Gotten", as in, We've Got it! Is this not the deliverer, born of the woman? Is this the serpent-crusher that we have waited for these long, painful years?

But by the time of Cain's brother's birth the gloom had descended again, for it must have become apparent that this was not the deliverer after all. They named this son Abel, "that which passes as a breath", indicating that they now knew that life itself is mortal, even a vapor.

<> <> <>

And in process of time it came to pass, that Cain brought of the fruit of the ground an offering unto the Lord And Abel, he also brought of the firstlings of his flock and of the fat thereof. And the Lord had respect unto Abel and to his offering But unto Cain and to his offering he had not respect. And Cain was very wroth, and his countenance fell. And the Lord said unto Cain, Why art thou wroth? and why is thy countenance fallen? If thou doest well, shalt thou not be accepted? and if thou doest not well, sin lieth at the door. And unto thee shall be his desire, and thou shalt rule over him (Genesis 4:3-7).

THE BROTHERS, CAIN AND Abel, each worshipped God. This God who once walked in the cool of the day in the garden with their parents, now had to be approached in a very specific way, due to the estrangement brought about by sin. Adam and Eve taught their sons the prescribed way to approach God as well as how and when to offer the God-appointed sacrifices. Thus both Cain and Abel knew that the worshipper could not come to God's altar empty-handed, for having been infected by sin from birth, no man is fit to approach the Holy God as he is in himself. God had appointed from the very beginning, a system of sacrificial worship.

From the time Adam and Eve looked with horror on the

carcass of the first slain animal, by whose fleece God had provided their garments, it became obvious that the sinners worthy of death could only be covered, or draw near to their God by way of substitutionary death. Blood must be spilled, for "the soul that sins shall die".

The theology of sacrifice is substitution. *The wages of sin is death.* Someone has to die for sin. Either the man himself, or the God-appointed substitute, but someone must die in order for fellowship with God to be possible. God's righteousness demands it.

When Abel drew near to the altar of God,[9] he brought in his hands the slain and bleeding carcass of the best and first of his flock. Tremblingly he approached with the broken body of the substitute, and by that offering made a statement such as this, **"I am but a sinner and deserve to die, O Holy Lord. I beseech you to receive this innocent substitute which You have appointed, to die in my place and cover my sins that I might live in Thy sight."**

He laid the offering on the altar, and somehow was allowed to see whether the offering was accepted or rejected.[10] In spite of Abel's sins, fellowship with God was established. His sins were covered and he would live.

When Cain drew near, he brought a different offering entirely. Thus he made a different theological statement. By bringing the produce of the ground, i.e., fruits and vegetables, Cain was saying to God something to this effect: **"I confess O Lord, that You are indeed my Creator, and have blessed the ground which has brought forth such fruit. I beseech You, receive this the work of my hands, from the ground which You have made."**

Cain was no atheist. He believed in God, and wanted to worship and acknowledge Him as Creator, and the giver of all good things, and rightly so. He was willing to take the place of a creature, even as a dependent on God. However

Cain refused to see himself as a sinner worthy of death, one who could only be saved by the God-appointed substitute. He presumed to approach the thrice Holy God without the shedding of blood!

> And almost all things are by the law purged with blood; and without shedding of blood is no remission (Hebrews 9:22).

Therefore Cain's offering didn't satisfy God. There was no sign of divine acceptance of Cain's worship. The Lord rejected Cain's offering in a very visible way.

Cain became angry, sullen, and even depressed. He had been shot down and he knew it. Abel had been accepted by God, but not Cain. This grieved and enraged him, but he said nothing.

Even when the LORD Himself confronted Cain with questions designed to bring him to a correction in his worship, and to provoke him to consider his own ways, Cain offered no response.

Why are you wroth, Cain? Why should you be depressed? You know what God requires and why He requires it. Why should you be angered? But Cain replied . . . nothing. He did not look within himself to ask why he should be angry, or depressed, or why does the divine teaching of the needed substitute bothered him so. He had nothing to say in response to the loving provocation of the LORD.

This time the LORD is direct in His query. *"If you do well will you not be accepted?"* In other words, Cain you know what you must do to come near to God. You know My terms of worship—you have to admit you are a sinner deserving of death in order to know My mercy and acceptance. But Cain's reply was . . . nothing.

So the LORD in mercy and forbearance warned him. He even pleaded with Cain, "Sin is a lion, Cain, that wants to devour you. But it can be overcome, Cain. You don't have to be destroyed, if you would but humble yourself."

But what did Cain have to say in response to the loving voice that sought to encourage him? Nothing.

Cain would not be the last sinner who ignored the gentle pleading of his Maker, shutting out the voice, killing the conscience until the solemn words of God spoken by Isaiah came to pass—

> I also will choose their delusions, and will bring their fears upon them; **because when I called, none did answer; when I spake, they did not hear**: but they did evil before mine eyes, and chose that in which I delighted not (Isaiah 66:4).

> And in process of time it came to pass, that Cain brought of the fruit of the ground an offering unto the Lord (Genesis 4:3).

Cain believed in God. Furthermore he worshipped him. The account of the first murder in human history, took place in the context of worship.

We would do well to consider the theology of Cain, for we are warned in the Book of Jude that in the last days many within the church and outside of it would "go in the way of Cain", plunging on into everlasting destruction.

> **Woe unto them! for they have gone in the way of Cain**, and ran greedily after the error of Balaam for reward, and perished in the gainsaying of Core. These are spots in your feasts of charity, when they feast with you, feeding themselves without fear: clouds they are without water, carried about of winds; trees whose fruit withereth, without fruit, twice dead, plucked up by the roots (Jude 11-12).

What exactly did Cain believe? What was the theology of the first murderer?

As stated earlier, Cain definitely believed in God. Furthermore, he was monotheistic, and understood the duty to worship God. I have no doubt that Cain acknowledged God as his Creator and as sustainer of all life, as evidenced by the nature of his sacrifice, the fruit of the ground blessed by God.

But Cain refused to acknowledge that he was a sinner, nor did he offer the appropriate God-ordained sacrifice—an innocent life—as a substitute. He refused to bring a bloody sacrifice to God. He simply balked at bringing this offering as a contrite and broken-hearted supplicant, seeking salvation.

Abel did, but not Cain.

Cain's approach to worship has a technical name, "Will Worship". After his own will and preference, he presumed to come to the Holy God on his own terms. His was a defiant religion of the flesh, a "works righteousness". He didn't like being considered a sinner and worthy of eternal destruction. He saw no need for a substitute. He would rely on himself, thus idealizing his own power and "goodness".

He would own God as Creator, but not as Redeemer.

Cain's insubordinate self-redemption and self-justification would become the preferred "respectable" religion of millions who would follow him. Those on the "way of Cain" are ever willing to acknowledge the Creator, and even to extol His benevolence or His other favorable attributes, but they adamantly balk at any suggestion of their own sinful condition, or any reference to the need of divine redemption, substitution, or the certainty of wrath and judgment!

This is the religion of the first murderer. It is a self-exalting will worship, self-justification, salvation by works, knowing God as Creator indeed, admitting His benevolent gift of life, but denying the Fall, redemption, and the certainty of hell.

Its origin is Cain but its thread is a constant of human history, leading all the way through to its final and fullest expression in the Antichrist, the ultimate "will worshipper", the man of sin, the son of perdition, "who opposes and exalts himself above all that is called God or is worshipped as God . . ." confessing ultimately that he himself is god!

The so-called "mainstream" Protestant churches have long since gone the way of Cain, for the most part, offering only a "social gospel" of good works, and "social justice". Abandoning the gospel they were brought into existence to bear witness to, what could justify the church's existence, other than a social service organization? They have abandoned the gospel revelation of the sin of man, and the need for repentance and personal rebirth. The idea of a God of holy wrath is an embarrassment to them. It is considered a barbaric throwback to primitive, unenlightened times. There will be no trembling hands bringing a bloody sacrifice to a Holy God in these churches now, only Cain's fruit.

But alas, within evangelicalism also, Cain's teaching has taken hold. Pastors, teachers, authors, and theologians have now emerged to deny the doctrine of propitiation, and also the concept which underlies and presupposes it, i.e., the wrath of God against all ungodliness and unrighteousness of men.

Popular books are being published which deny the doctrine of eternal punishment (hell) in the name of the only attribute modern apostates will ever allow in God: love. An evangelical church is "emerging" which emphasizes ritual, sensual religious experience, psychology, and humanistic love, but which adamantly opposes the doctrines of a Holy God of wrath and justice, which in no way negates His mercy and grace.

But the Most High God rejected the offering of Cain.

If there is a "way of Cain" as the apostles warned us, surely there is a contrasting way of Abel. As Erich Sauer points out in his *Dawn of World Redemption*—

> [It is] the humble acknowledgement that sin demands death, the reliance of the guilty on the sacrifice appointed by God himself, the enduring of persecution for the sake of the eternal goal, the expectation of the triumph of the Divine Redemption through the woman's seed.[11]

Cain's way will soon perish. It leads to the Antichrist and to judgment and hell itself, for it is ever rejected of God. But Abel, though like the ultimate Abel, the Messiah, who also was persecuted and even slain, attains eternal life!

<> <> <>

But unto Cain and to his offering he had not respect. And Cain was very wroth, and his countenance fell. And the Lord said unto Cain, Why art thou wroth? and why is thy countenance fallen? If thou doest well, shalt thou not be accepted? and if thou doest not well, sin lieth at the door. And unto thee shall be his desire, and thou shalt rule over him. And Cain talked with Abel his brother: and it came to pass, when they were in the field, that Cain rose up against Abel his brother, and slew him (Genesis 4:5-8).

CAIN OFFERED NO RESPONSE to the entreaties of God. Rather, he abode in the grip of his own anger and depression.

The Most High God would have helped him to examine his own rebellious heart, and to realize that the way to communion with God had been clearly marked, and that Cain could conquer the sin, which stalked him. If he would but humble himself and "do well", God would bless him with divine acceptance also, as He did Abel his brother.

Was it Abel himself by whom the Most High spoke to Cain? Or was it that Abel's own submission to God was a constant witness to Cain's conscience that he was not right with God? We don't know for sure the answers to those questions. We know only that Cain slew Abel in a field.

The apostle John gives us the divine explanation in 1 John 3:11-12:

> For this is the message that ye heard from the beginning, that we should love one another. Not as Cain, who was of that wicked one, and slew his brother. And wherefore slew he him? Because his own works were evil, and his brother's righteous.

Why did Cain slay Abel? John gives us two reasons, 1) Because he was of the wicked one. Cain was of a spiritual affinity with Satan. He proved himself to be of the "seed of the serpent" in the sense that he shared in the rebellion and hatred of God that Satan has.

2) Because his own works were evil and his brother's were righteousness. In other words, jealousy. He didn't necessarily want to be righteous, but he resented his brother's righteousness.

The Greek word for "slay", *esphaxon,* in 1 John 3:12, is a word that has sacrificial implications. It means to kill by cutting the throat. It is similar to the word which refers to "the Lamb slain . . ." in Revelation, *sphazo.*

In other words, there is a sacrificial sense to the description of Cain's murder of Abel.

Cain wouldn't submit to offering the God-appointed substitute for his sin. He saw no need for such a humbling posture. Cain was going to come to God on his own terms, and in his own righteousness.

But all sin demands a sacrifice; someone has to pay! Therefore Cain ended up offering up Abel his brother, not to the Most High God of course, but to his own wounded pride and evil conscience. Cain made Abel pay with his life.

And such it is with all false religion, no matter how seemingly benign. If they will not be reconciled to God by the God-appointed sacrifice of Christ, sooner or later they prove to be violent. This is true of Hinduism, (which has a violent, murderous side to it), Islam, animism, ancestor worship, and it is even true of apostate Christianity. Cain always slays Abel!

I once witnessed to a Muslim on a plane, who proudly asserted, "We Muslims need no sacrifice." I then quietly asked him why everywhere in the world Islam spreads, innocent blood is spilt as a consequence. Why do the Muslims perpetually make war on infidels? The false religion that refuses the God-appointed sacrifice, ends up making others pay in blood!

The Islamic suicide bomber who boards an Israeli bus full of mothers, fathers, children, old people, is told by his religion, that by mercilessly blowing them to pieces in the name of Allah, he can vault over the carnage of broken men, women and children, into a pornographic paradise forever!

Likewise, the mainline denominations of liberal Protestantism, which have supposedly outgrown "barbaric" notions such as the wrath of God, hell, Jesus as a propitiation, and salvation by the shed blood of Jesus, are almost universally pro-choice in the abortion debate!

The story of Cain teaches us among other things, that when a religion denies the teaching of substitution, and the need for the God-appointed sacrifice for sin, and the just wrath of God that presupposes it, someone else will have to be made to pay for sin, in some manner.

Was killing an animal, as God taught them to, and approaching God with a propitiation offering, somehow "beneath" the dignity of Cain's religion? But Cain did offer his own righteous brother up, as a sacrifice to his own hatred, envy and jealousy. The man too good for "blood atonement" ended up being a murderer.

Is the "old fashioned" religion of fundamentalist Christianity beneath the modern humanistic sensibilities of liberal Christianity? Liberals have a problem with wrath, judgment, the cross as a propitiation, Jesus as a substitute in judgment, but no problem with abortion, homosexuality and feminism! This is the way of Cain!

Evangelism which emphasizes concepts such as the wrath of God, judgment, hell, the gravity of sin, and courtroom language of "justification" and "condemnation", is now being set aside by many as being too harsh, off-putting, and even condemning, (a "turn off" to the unsaved), and is being replaced by a "relational" emphasis instead, by the modern Cains of our day.

The divine sentence was pronounced upon Cain, and it elicited a heartfelt response from him in a way that God's urgings and pleadings before and after the murder didn't. The import of this sentence deeply hurt Cain. It frightened and exasperated him to the point that he who had previously ignored God's tender calls to repentance, now openly pleaded with God.

I have highlighted in the verses above, what I believe the real issue was and why it elicited such an anguished response from the first recorded murderer and will worshipper.

The divine punishment set upon Cain had to do with his relationship to the earth. Remember that Cain was a farmer. The earth had once yielded her bounty (by God's blessing) to Cain. But it would no longer do so. Why wouldn't the earth bring forth the bounty to Cain? The earth had already "opened her mouth" to receive the shed blood of Abel, Cain's murdered brother.

In God's dealing, the earth can be made to be morally sensitive. Centuries later the Israelites were warned that should they defect and follow the abominations of the Canaanites, the Holy Land itself would vomit them out of its boundaries.

> Defile not ye yourselves in any of these things: for in all these the nations are defiled which I cast out before you: And the land is defiled: therefore I do visit the iniquity thereof upon it, and the land itself vomiteth out her inhabitants (Leviticus 18:24-25).

When Cain complained that God has "driven" him out from the earth, the Hebrew word used, *geirashti*, is the same word used in other places in Scripture for divorce. God divorced Cain from the earth as a punishment for murder!

The consequences of this rejection of Cain by the earth itself were immense and far-reaching. No longer would Cain have a settled place to live, nor would he be able by agriculture to provide sustenance for himself. He was sentenced to be a "fugitive and a vagabond". He would no longer be "grounded", in the sense of being able to have a permanent settled place. Cain would ever be restless, a perpetual exile, and alienated from working the land, thus dependant on others for the sustenance which he himself once derived from the earth.

This was a serious situation in itself, but there was another dimension added to Cain's pain. The reality that murder was now conceivable to the fallen children of Adam, made the world of Cain's exile a frightening, threatening place.

Cain knew that his act had destroyed what sense of security existed among the children of Adam. He had done the unthinkable! He had crossed a threshold when he killed his brother. Who knew what forces of hatred vengeance were now released in the hearts of his other fallen brothers and sisters?

Who hasn't experienced something similar in our increasingly dark modern-day? We once left our doors unlocked at night, and trusted friends and neighbors for the most part. But that was a thousand grisly newspaper stories ago!

Cain created a new hostile and distrustful world, not only for himself but for everyone. So in self-pity he pleaded with the Judge of the earth for a concession . . .

> . . . it shall come to pass, that every one that findeth me shall slay me. And the Lord said unto him, Therefore whosoever slayeth Cain, vengeance shall be taken on him sevenfold. And the Lord set a mark upon Cain, lest any finding him should kill him.

In mercy the Lord assured Cain of this protection, a special mark of God, and a warning to anyone who would violate Cain's life. God would execute "sevenfold vengeance" on whoever would kill Cain.

How does anyone suffer seven times as much as the person they murdered? What could be worse than death itself?

What God was doing here is assuring all of humanity that physical death itself is not the end for anyone, and that there are sanctions that go beyond this life into the next.

"Sevenfold vengeance" is another way of saying, "full and eternal suffering" after death—what we now know of as hell and the lake of fire—to the one who would dare to slay Cain.

In Luke 12, Jesus alluded to this very contrast between physical and eternal vengeance, when He warned us not to fear him who could only kill the body, but to fear the one who has power to "cast body and soul into hell!"

> And I say unto you my friends, Be not afraid of them that kill the body, and after that have no more that they can do. But I will forewarn you whom ye shall fear: Fear him, which after he hath killed hath power to cast into hell; yea, I say unto you, Fear him.(Luke 12:4-5)

<> <> <>

> *And Cain went out from the presence of the Lord, and dwelt in the land of Nod, on the east of Eden. And Cain knew his wife; and she conceived, and bare Enoch: and he builded a city, and called the name of the city, after the name of his son, Enoch (Genesis 4:16-17).*

THE STORY OF CAIN: his rejected worship, the murder of his brother, consequently ,his sentence to be a vagabond on earth, and the city he built, is one of the primary lessons of the entire Bible. The God of the Bible wants us to consider the deeper lessons of this narrative, placing it prominently as the fourth chapter of Scripture, after Creation and the Fall.

Jesus and the apostles bring up Cain again. Jesus, makes mention of the slaying of Abel, (He doesn't mention Cain by name), as the prototypical martyrdom. The inspired author of the Book of Hebrews contrasted the faith of Abel with the unbelief of Cain, in the faith chapter. The apostle John sets Cain and Christ out as the only two alternative humanities.

> For this is the message that ye heard from the beginning, that we should love one another. **Not as Cain, who was of that wicked one, and slew his brother.** And wherefore slew he him? Because his

own works were evil, and his brother's righteous
... Hereby perceive we the love of God, because he
laid down his life for us: and we ought to lay down
our lives for the brethren (1 John 3:12, 16).

Finally, Jude warns of those false converts and will worshippers who have "gone in the way of Cain". The lessons of
this story go far beyond the surface moral caution against
envy and murder. The story of Cain and his line is designed
to teach us something about all of fallen humanity, regard-
ing our relationship to God, our environment and ourselves.

We note that Cain had no response to the living, personal God, when God was warning him against sin, and afterwards when God was calling him to repentance. Other than
a sarcastic, cynical retort, *"Am I my brother's keeper?"*, Cain
had nothing to say in reply to God's pleadings.

But when the divine sentence was passed, basically "di-
vorcing" Cain from the earth for life, cursing any attempts
at farming, and making him a homeless exile, Cain responded with passionate pleading. He was afraid that someone
would take vengeance upon him.

The murder of his brother had infused the world with
fear, and insecurity. If something as sacred as life can be tak-
en with impunity, there was nothing else that was unthinkable. Cain was frightened for his own life.

But in mercy upon the open rebel, God put a mark upon
Cain, an assurance that any who violated Cain would suffer
divine vengeance even beyond physical death. Cain was under God's protection even in his homeless wandering. But
that mark was not enough for Cain, for he chose not to believe in it.

So Cain departed from "the presence of the Lord". He
would never know whether the mark would have protected
him or not. It didn't seem adequate to him; therefore he
simply left God, not physically of course, but spiritually and
morally.

The convicted murderer could have chosen to submit to God's sentence, and put himself under the mercy and protection of God, but he wanted some better security than God's "mark". Also, in spite of the divine sentence passed upon him, he longed for rest from his wanderings.

Cain left the presence of the Lord and began a new life, a life without the God who had condemned him. He would himself define life, beauty and meaning without God. He came to love in the land of Nod. Ironically, "Nod" means "wanderings". Cain had gone into restlessness. Even if he "settled down" he could never truly settle down, for he was sentenced by God to go nowhere, and to find nothing, and to have perpetual insecurity.

"East of Eden", away from God's presence and the memory of the paradise, Cain set about making his own life. He tried to secure himself and escape from his wanderings by building the world's first city.

The name of the world's first city is also the name of Cain's son, Enoch, or "initiation". Cain was initiating a new (godless) way of life, as well as a new (godless) security, and a completely new (godless) sense of rootedness. Here the God-estranged wanderer could settle in, take root and consider himself at home.

But could Cain (and all he represents) truly stop his endless wandering in the city which he had made? Was he finally able to be at rest? Did the city give him the sense of permanence and security that he craved? Was the godless exile at home there? Was it possible to remake a secure world without God?

We are currently living in the final stages of Cain's grand experiment. For the Bible tells us that the real story of human development is the contrast and strivings of two cities, the doomed city of man and the ultimately triumphant "city of God"!

In that day shall this song be sung in the land of Judah; **We have a strong city**; salvation will God appoint for walls and bulwarks. Open ye the gates, that the righteous nation which keepeth the truth may enter in. Thou wilt keep him in perfect peace, whose mind is stayed on thee: because he trusteth in thee. Trust ye in the Lord for ever: for in the Lord Jehovah is everlasting strength: For he bringeth down them that dwell on high; **the lofty city, he layeth it low**; he layeth it low, even to the ground; he bringeth it even to the dust (Isaiah 26:1-5).

<> <> <>

And Cain went out from the presence of the Lord, and dwelt in the land of Nod, on the east of Eden. And Cain knew his wife; and she conceived, and bare Enoch: and he builded a city, and called the name of the city, after the name of his son, Enoch. And unto Enoch was born Irad: and Irad begat Mehujael: and Mehujael begat Methusael: and Methusael begat Lamech. And Lamech took unto him two wives: the name of the one was Adah, and the name of the other Zillah. And Adah bare Jabal: he was the father of such as dwell in tents, and of such as have cattle. And his brother's name was Jubal: he was the father of all such as handle the harp and organ. And Zillah, she also bare Tubalcain, an instructer of every artificer in brass and iron: and the sister of Tubalcain was Naamah. And Lamech said unto his wives, Adah and Zillah, Hear my voice; ye wives of Lamech, hearken unto my speech: for I have slain a man to my wounding, and a young man to my hurt. If Cain shall be avenged sevenfold, truly Lamech seventy and sevenfold (Genesis 4:16-24).

WE ARE GIVEN IN few words, a picture of the overall development of humanity in the generations that followed Cain's "New Start" (the city, Enoch), away from the presence of God.

The direction that the entire civilizational line of Cain took, was one of self-redemption. Indeed they acknowledged that there was a curse upon the earth, and that men were no longer in the "garden of delight", and in Cain's case especially, the earth no longer yielded her goodness.

Therefore, through hard work and knowledge, they would overcome the curse. And by the development of the city, and through advances in agriculture, the seed of Cain could create their own "garden of Eden" with all of its comforts and security, but without any acknowledgment of God. Human unity and ingenuity would be able to achieve these breakthroughs.

This is why the Holy Spirit chose to highlight three sons of Lamech, each leaders in areas of development undertaken by the seed of Cain. Though fallen, the Cainites still bore the image of God and the God-given powers of dominion over creation. The mandate was still upon all men to "subdue" the earth.

First, we meet the nomadic Jabal, who led the way into advancement in animal husbandry. Secondly, the artist Jubal developed the fine arts through the invention of new musical instruments. Finally, Tubal-Cain, the metallurgist, was the father of the smith's trade.

Thus the line of Cain sustained itself through the fine arts, music, technology, and agricultural development. Animal science, metallurgy, and advances in building and weaponry were just some of the trades which developed and were put to the service of Cain's project, i.e., building a secure civilization, overcoming the curse, making a meaningful life on this earth, to the exclusion of God as Creator or Redeemer.

The flourishing of new forms of music, poetry, painting and prose, and beautiful instruments soothed the troubled consciences of the God-estranged Cainites.

Jabal, with his multiplying herds and his hardier breeds, provided a steady supply of milk, meat, wool and leather. And Tubal-Cain's alloys gave the community the weapons needed to defend themselves, and the tools needed to subdue the resistant earth.[12]

Was Cain condemned by God to wander? There was no need for that, for his city provided him with a settled place, in spite of God's judgment. He would not be a vagabond, (at least externally)! Cain needed no "mark of God" to defend him; he now had fortified walls around himself.

Thus did Cain's "new start", his *Enoch* civilization, set itself directly against the Word of God and sought to even mitigate the curse and reverse the fall by technology, the arts and sciences, without any reference to the God of Creation.

The only alternative to Cain's "east of Eden" community at that time was a small and less advanced line of human development, the line of Seth. They didn't rapidly develop technology,[13] for the trend among them was the patient waiting underneath the curse for the relief that was promised by the "seed of the woman".

We can see Seth's mindset by the name of his son, "Enos," which means frailty. By this Seth acknowledged the chastening hand of God and humbled himself under it, knowing that the ultimate triumph over the curse would come by God's hand and at His time.

The other prominent characteristic among the "Sethite" civilization which developed was that in those days they began to organize themselves to "call upon the name of the LORD".

<> <> <>

> *And Adam knew his wife again; and she bare a son, and called his name Seth: For God, said she, hath appointed me another seed instead of Abel, whom Cain slew. And to Seth, to him also there was born a son; and he called his name Enos: then began men to call upon the name of the Lord (Genesis 4:25-26).*

BUT A DISTURBING PICTURE emerges from the sparse snapshot of family life as it came to develop among the Cainites. In the case of Lamech, the seventh from Adam, we see that the primal law of marriage to one woman had already been cast aside as irrelevant, for Lamech was a polygamist.

> Hear my voice; ye wives of Lamech, hearken unto my speech: for I have slain a man to my wounding, and a young man to my hurt. If Cain shall be avenged sevenfold, truly Lamech seventy and sevenfold.

These are the earliest recorded words in Scripture of a song, but rather than praises to God, we hear the blasphemous boasts of a violent, vengeful "hero" comparing his own violent retribution for any perceived slight, to the merciful concession God offered his frightened forefather Cain. "If Cain be avenged sevenfold, Lamech, seventy and sevenfold!"

As G. H. Pember so aptly described,

> The history of the Cainites begins with a murder, and ends with praise of a murder. In its seventh number, everything is forgotten; with music, social amenities, luxury, and display everything

is benumbed. The curse of loneliness is changed into city life, the curse of being unsettled into love of travel, the bad conscience into heroism, which makes the remembrance of the curse of God's ancestors only a support of one's own God blaspheming self consciousness. Thus all is pleasure, splendor, entwined and crowned with the flower of human wit and the soul's creative power, and poetic art.[14]

Can you see that this is also a description of our current world? Have not our increases in technology, advances in the arts, in agriculture and defense caused us also to forget that this world is cursed and that thus it is not our permanent home?

Have we also not seen a systematic dismantling of our once Christian culture? The utter rejection by this terminal generation of the primal law of marriage, the role of male and female, the sanctity of life, and civility and society? Do we not now hear "artists" celebrating all that is base, violent, nihilistic and blasphemous? Where does the Cainite civilization end, but in the divinely ordained destruction of the Flood?

7

The Generations of Adam

This is the book of the generations of Adam. In the day that God created man, in the likeness of God made he him; Male and female created he them; and blessed them, and called their name Adam, in the day when they were created. And Adam lived an hundred and thirty years, and begat a son in his own likeness, and after his image; and called his name Seth: And the days of Adam after he had begotten Seth were eight hundred years: and he begat sons and daughters: And all the days that Adam lived were nine hundred and thirty years: and he died (Genesis 5:1-5).

THE BOOK OF GENESIS is divided into ten sections, called, *toledoth*, which is the Hebrew word for "generations". Each section opens with the expression, "These are the generations *(toledoth)* of . . ." The divisions are—

Genesis 2:4 (the heavens and the earth)

Genesis 5:1(Adam's descendents)

Genesis 6:9 (Noah)

Genesis 10:11 (Shem, Ham, and Japheth)

Genesis 11:10 (Shem)

Genesis 11:27 (Terah)

Genesis 25:12 (Ishmael)

Genesis 25:19 (Isaac)

Genesis 36:1 (Esau)

Genesis 37:2 (Jacob)

Note that God created Adam in His own image and likeness, as we were told earlier in the Creation account. But by the time Adam begat a son, it was "in his own (Adam's) likeness" that he was begotten. Adam was made "in the image of God" but Seth was born in the "likeness and image of Adam".

All of Adam's children indeed bear the *"image and likeness of God"*. However there is a sense in which we all inherit the "image of Adam" also. As children of Adam, we are born with a fallen nature, which is already corrupted and estranged from God. As the first of the human race, Adam bore in himself the whole race, representing us, in the garden.

When Adam fell away from God, we also fell away in him, and consequently we bear in our unregenerate nature the fallen and corrupted "image of Adam". Thus King David laments in the Penitential Psalm,

> Behold, I was shapen in iniquity; and in sin did my mother conceive me (Psalm 51:5).

The psalmist is not castigating his mother and father, nor the circumstances of his conception, rather King David is in horror realizing the totality of iniquity in his life, that he has been a sinner through and through since his very birth!

There is a mysterious solidarity of the human race. "From one blood He made us all". We were all "in Adam" and share not only the dignity inherent in being made "in the image of God", but we also have a share in the fall and shame of Adam, and in his estrangement from God.

The New Testament bears this out, especially in the teaching of Paul, who revealed that in God's economy there are two representative men—Adam and/or Christ, (who is called, the last Adam), with whom the entire human race is alternately identified.

> For since by man came death, by man came also the resurrection of the dead. For as in Adam all die, even so in Christ shall all be made alive (1 Corinthians 15:21-22).

By virtue of the first birth, we all bear the fallen nature of Adam, the transgressor. All of humanity shares in his shame, folly, corruption and rebellion, and all of us have personally repeated his defection from God, for we are, "by nature, children of wrath . . ." (Ephesians 2).

But there is another Adam, the last Adam, who by His death and resurrection has made it possible for this fallen race to have a new beginning, by offering each of us a new nature.

> And so it is written, The first man Adam was made a living soul; the last Adam was made a quickening spirit. Howbeit that was not first which is spiritual, but that which is natural; and afterward that which is spiritual. The first man is of the earth, earthy; the second man is the Lord from heaven. As is the earthy, such are they also that are earthy: and as is the heavenly, such are they also that are heavenly (1 Corinthians 15:45-48).

But all who are born of Adam, must die, so Genesis 5 is, among other things, a litany of death. The generations of Adam are living out the stern warning that God gave Adam in the beginning, *"The day you eat of this tree, you shall die"* or literally, *"In dying you shall be dying."*

We have been examining the two contrasting lines, which developed from among Adam's children. Cain, the world's first will worshipper and murderer, set out "east of Eden", away from the presence of the Lord, to inaugurate a new start for mankind. The city of Enoch and its subsequent civilization would develop out of it.

Cainite civilization quickly advanced, exercising dominion over the earth in spite of its God-estrangement; building cities, developing technology, metallurgy, agriculture, animal husbandry, music and the arts. They sought to mitigate the curse upon the earth, without repentance. There was no turning to God; rather they relied on human ingenuity, intelligence, strength, and innovation to make a life for themselves in this world.

The names of some of the great innovators survive from this people—Enoch, for whom the first city was named, and Tubal-Cain, Jubal and Jabal, who developed arts, science and agriculture. There are prominent women named also, such as Adah and Zillhah, the wives of Lamech.

What about the other line? How did it fare with the seed of Seth, the substitute son, who followed the faith of the murdered Abel? We have already been told that it was in the days of Seth, at the birth of his son Enos (Frail), that men first began to gather together to call upon the name of the LORD.

> And Adam knew his wife again; and she bare a son, and called his name Seth: For God, said she, hath appointed me another seed instead of Abel, whom Cain slew. And to Seth, to him also there

was born a son; and he called his name Enos:
then began men to call upon the name of the Lord
(Genesis 4:25-26).

As Pember states of the contrast between the two lines,

> But when we turn to Seth's posterity, the scene
> changes. Envyings, strifes, and deeds of license
> and violence are no longer before us: our ears
> cease to to be assailed with the lowings of herds,
> the strains of soft music used for the soothing of
> uneasy consciences; the clatter of the anvil, the
> vauntings of proud boasters, and all of the min-
> gled din which arises from a world living without
> God, and struggling to overpower His curse ...[15]

The Cainite line was definitely what we could call
worldly. They had launched out on their own to create a
civilization without God or His input. Being men made in
the image of God, they utilized their mastery over creation
through technology. But being fallen creatures, their use of
technology and the arts could not compensate for the violence, hatred, and lust, which raged in their hearts.

But in the other line, that of Seth,

> ... we see a poor people and afflicted; toiling day
> after day to procure food from the ungenial soil,
> according to their God's appointment, patiently
> waiting till He should be gracious, and humbly
> acknowledging his chastening hand upon them.
> They have no share in earth's history; that is
> entirely made up of Cainites. As strangers and
> pilgrims they abstain from fleshly lusts. They
> build no cities, they invent no arts, they devise no
> amusements, They are not mindful of that coun-
> try in which they live, but seek a better, that is a
> heavenly... [16]

But this chapter isn't only about the inheritance of a fallen nature, and centuries of birth and death and the curse. God is good, and where sin abounds, grace does much more abound. We come next to an amazing prophecy of hope hidden in the names of the line of Seth.

The sequence of names in this genealogy itself is a prophecy. Each name has a meaning, and when the meanings are put together, a message from God emerges which speaks to all of those whose faith has made them into pilgrims, seeking a "city whose builder and maker is God", like the children of Seth.

Adam = man

Seth = appointed

Enos = mortal

Cainan (Kenan) = sorrow (elegy)

Mehalaleel = the blessed God

Jared = descending

Enoch = initiate

Methuselah = his death shall bring

Lamech = the despairing

Noah = rest

Thus the very genealogy of Adam through the line of Seth is a prophetic pronouncement of salvation. "Man [was] appointed [to] mortal sorrow, [but] the blessed God shall come down, teaching [that] His death shall bring the despairing rest!"

Meanings of the Names in Genesis 5

A few of the names of this godly line stand out, particularly at the end, as the line of Seth began itself to fade into accommodation and ultimate dissolution into Cain's line and fall under divine judgment.

Enoch was the first of a line of four prophets. He is said in Hebrews 11 to have *"walked with God, and was not, for God took him".* In an age of unbelief, defection and exponentially accumulating evil, this man walked with God, preaching righteousness, and warning men of the judgment to come. But suddenly Enoch was raptured!

Enoch had previously been given a vision, not of the Deluge, but of the final return of the Lord in glory and of the judgment upon the ungodly.

> And Enoch also, the seventh from Adam, prophesied of these, saying, Behold, the Lord cometh with ten thousands of his saints, To execute judgment upon all, and to convince all that are ungodly among them of all their ungodly deeds which they have ungodly committed, and of all their hard speeches which ungodly sinners have spoken against him (Jude 14-15).

The Son of Enoch, Methuselah, had a name, which was itself a prophecy. "When he goes it comes . . ." or "his death shall bring . . ." Bring what? The flood that Enoch, Methuselah and Lamech had been warning about came to pass on the very year that Methuselah died.

But Methuselah had this distinction also; he lived longer than anyone else had ever lived, 969 years. This is a testimony to the patience and love of God, who *"is not willing that any should perish but that all should come to repentance".* As long as people could behold Methuselah, they could know there was yet time to turn to God in humble repentance.

Lamech named his Son, "Noah", which means "rest",

prophesying that,

> . . . This same shall comfort us concerning our work and toil of our hands, because of the ground which the Lord hath cursed (Genesis 5:29).

> And Enoch lived sixty and five years, and begat Methuselah: And Enoch walked with God after he begat Methuselah three hundred years, and begat sons and daughters: And all the days of Enoch were three hundred sixty and five years: And Enoch walked with God: and he was not; for God took him (Genesis 5: 21-24).

We are given a contrast, in Genesis 4-5, between these two lines of humanity, (for they currently flow together in our world also), by highlighting an example from the seventh generation of each. For by seven generations the seed of each line comes to its fullest expression.

In the case of the seventh from Adam through the line of Cain, we come to Lamech.

> And Lamech said unto his wives, Adah and Zillah, Hear my voice; ye wives of Lamech, hearken unto my speech: for I have slain a man to my wounding, and a young man to my hurt. If Cain shall be avenged sevenfold, truly Lamech seventy and sevenfold (Genesis 4:23-24).

How far will God allow godlessness to develop? Where does it end up? What does a society of Lamechs look like? Cain was a will worshipper, but at the beginning he at least acknowledged God as Creator. The first dispute involved approved or disapproved worship.

But Cain leads to Lamech. And Lamech led to the destruction of the Flood.

By the time of Lamech, note the fact that the primal law

of marriage is completely disregarded, and that the first recorded song is a blasphemous boast of Lamech's prowess, that his vengeance of a perceived slight would be greater than the Holy God's eternal sentence on transgressors.

Our own Cain generation has long forgotten the Judeo-Christian roots which once nourished us. Thirty years ago could we have dreamed of the degraded society which we now inhabit? The fact that there would even be such a subject as "Gay marriage" in our lifetime would have been unthinkable to many of us thirty years ago.

Can it be true that America has come upon the fortieth year of legal abortion and has killed more than 50 million of our most innocent? What has happened to us? How we have died! How we have rotted and corrupted! How ugly our once beautiful civilization has become!!!

But alongside the tares—the God-defying "seed of the serpent" and the self-magnifying, violent, boasting Cain culture—there also developed the wheat, the line of Seth. The contrasting seventh from Adam representative of this generation was a preacher of righteousness named Enoch. He saw a vision of the final judgment and of the coming of the Lord in glory.

> And Enoch also, the seventh from Adam, prophesied of these, saying, Behold, the Lord cometh with ten thousands of his saints, To execute judgment upon all, and to convince all that are ungodly among them of all their ungodly deeds which they have ungodly committed, and of all their hard speeches which ungodly sinners have spoken against him (Jude 13-14).

To Enoch also was shown the fact that the Flood would come in the final year of his son, Methuselah. The name Methuselah is itself a prophecy, meaning, "his death shall bring", and the Flood came the year he died. This is a testi-

mony to the longsuffering of God, for Methuselah is recorded as being the oldest person to ever live, 969 years!

Centuries later the apostle Peter would point out to us
the reason for the long delay in divine judgment, that the
story of Methuselah underscores.

> But, beloved, be not ignorant of this one thing,
> that one day is with the Lord as a thousand years,
> and a thousand years as one day. The Lord is not
> slack concerning his promise, as some men count
> slackness; but is longsuffering to us-ward, not
> willing that any should perish, but that all should
> come to repentance (2 Peter 3:8-9).

Where does the line of Abel and Seth lead? What is the
fullest expression of this line in the seventh generation
from Adam? That longsuffering generation which was not
as flamboyant as the Cainites, were instead mocked and rid-
iculed. They could not point so much to the "great men" in
their midst or to the famous women, but instead humbly
gathered to "call upon the LORD" in the day of apostasy and
defection.

It leads to Enoch, who walked with God, preaching,
teaching, warning, admonishing for three hundred and six-
ty five years! The godly line, the humble "seed of the woman", which extended from Abel who was murdered, through
the line of worshippers unto Enoch, the seventh from Adam.
What happened to him?

He was raptured.

As Hebrews reminds us, it matters not so much whether
we are slain like Abel, or raptured as Enoch was. What matters is the testimony of saving faith within.

> By faith Abel offered unto God a more excellent
> sacrifice than Cain, by which he obtained wit-
> ness that he was righteous, God testifying of his
> gifts: and by it he being dead yet speaketh. By

faith Enoch was translated that he should not see death; and was not found, because God had translated him: for before his translation he had this testimony, that he pleased God (Hebrews 11:4-5).

8

The Days of Noah

And it came to pass, when men began to multiply on the face of the earth, and daughters were born unto them, That the sons of God saw the daughters of men that they were fair; and they took them wives of all which they chose. And the Lord said, My spirit shall not always strive with man, for that he also is flesh: yet his days shall be an hundred and twenty years (Genesis 6:1-3).

And as it was in the days of Noe, so shall it be also in the days of the Son of man. They did eat, they drank, they married wives, they were given in marriage, until the day that Noah entered into the ark, and the flood came, and destroyed them all (Luke 17:26-27).

JESUS SAID THAT THE time of His coming would be "as in the days of Noah". The way it was at the end of the family lines of Cain and of Seth, i.e., the last days of the generations immediately following Adam will be duplicated in the last days of our present dispensation. Genesis 4-6 are eschatological, because the conditions will be repeated.

What happened in the Days of Noah? What were the

conditions that led up to the Flood? There were several signal factors that led up to the cataclysmic execution of the wrath of God upon the earth upon all but eight souls. I will list them as best as possible, using only the biblical text.

1) **A population explosion**—*men began to multiply on the face of the earth.*

Physical conditions on the earth were optimal for growth and long life. People in the post-Flood world wonder about anyone living for 700, 800 or even 900 years, but remember that a canopy covered the earth, shielding men from direct sunlight, ensuring maximum growing conditions. People would have been quite healthy and fertile for a long time.

But with the growth of population, came intensification of sin. Cities tend to compound the human resistance to God. People influence each other, bolstering one another in evil habits, acts of daring, cutting edged defiance.

Age also would be a factor. Imagine a life of hundreds of years of accumulated wickedness, and long practiced God resistance. How hard the heart would become after a point! How toxic an influence an evildoer would be, should he be allowed to continue unto the hundreds of years!

2) **Breakthroughs in the sciences, technology, and the arts.**

We have already discussed the sons of Cain, and their innovations in mitigating the effects of the curse, rendering life easier, affording leisure, and most important of all, tending to give the impression that life can be lived without the acknowledgement of God.

3) **The willful disregard for marriage.**

Marriage was designed and ordained of God, to be between one man and one woman for life. It is one of the primal laws, the "everlasting covenant" Isaiah laments about.

> The earth also is defiled under the inhabitants thereof; because they have transgressed the laws, changed the ordinance, **broken the everlasting covenant** (Isaiah 24:5).

In a debate with His theological enemies about marriage and divorce, Jesus takes us back, not to the provisional laws of marriage and divorce in the law of Moses, but to the very beginning, defining marriage.

> And he answered and said unto them, Have ye not read, that he which made them at the beginning made them male and female, And said, For this cause shall a man leave father and mother, and shall cleave to his wife: and they twain shall be one flesh? Wherefore they are no more twain, but one flesh. What therefore God hath joined together, let not man put asunder (Matthew 19:3-6).

But today, as in the days of Noah, as seen in the example of Lamech, we see that the very concept of marriage has been perverted and even forsaken.

So, too, had the roles of men and women as assigned by God. Lamech's two wives and daughter are known by name. Lamech's wives, Ada, "ornament, or beauty", Zillah, "the shady", (on account of her tresses?) and also his daughter Naama, "loveliness" were renown, as their names indicate, for their outward beauty and sensual attractiveness.

But in the godly line before the Flood, women took no prominent place. No woman was known by name of Seth's line, nor do we know the names of the wives of Noah, Methuselah, Enoch. Perhaps this was a reflection of the "meek and quite spirit" the apostle Peter told us, is so precious to God.

Likewise, ye wives, be in subjection to your own husbands; that, if any obey not the word, they also may without the word be won by the conversation of the wives; While they behold your chaste conversation coupled with fear. Whose adorning let it not be that outward adorning of plaiting the hair, and of wearing of gold, or of putting on of apparel; But let it be the hidden man of the heart, in that which is not corruptible, even the ornament of a meek and quiet spirit, which is in the sight of God of great price. For after this manner in the old time the holy women also, who trusted in God, adorned themselves, being in subjection unto their own husbands (1 Peter 3:1-5).

4) Another sign of the days of Noah, is **the overall rejection of the call to repentance and faith in God.**

Centuries had passed, in which men such as Enos led the congregation to call upon the name of the LORD Redeemer, and those fiery preachers such as Enoch, Lamech, Methselah, called men to repentance in view of the coming judgment. But by the time of the days of Noah, what do we find? Only a congregation of eight people was aware of what was coming.

There could have been millions or perhaps even a billion on the earth, but by the time of the Flood, there were only eight who believed. This is because the fifth sign of the days of Noah is . . .

5) **The obliteration of separation between the line of Cain and the line of Seth.**

We see little distinction, in our day, between the children of God and those of this Age. Those earliest centuries saw the diminishment of the line of Seth, which succumbed to the licentious, unbelieving spirit of its own age. Gradually the "congregation" became just another worldly institution, making no apparent difference in the people's lives. The organized services of calling upon the LORD descended into ritual, and perhaps imperceptibly the light flickered, sputtered and all but died out.

Cainite and Sethite alike had more and more in common, as they commenced with business as usual; they married, gave in marriage, built houses, invested in future business, had children, ate at restaurants, went to theaters, and lived as though there was no God to fear.

The "church" had become the world. There were perhaps services or functions, but there would be no messages of judgment, no fear of God, no confrontation with the increasingly evil practices which abounded around them, perhaps a few moral lessons here and there, but nothing too radical . . . (They wouldn't want to be identified with that crazy Noah!) . . . until the end came . . .

> The earth also was corrupt before God, and the earth was filled with violence. And God looked upon the earth, and, behold, it was corrupt; for all flesh had corrupted his way upon the earth. And God said unto Noah, The end of all flesh is come before me; for the earth is filled with violence through them; and, behold, I will destroy them with the earth (Genesis 6:12-13).

> But as the days of Noah were, so shall also the coming of the Son of man be. For as in the days that were before the flood they were eating and drinking, marrying and giving in marriage, until the day that Noe entered into the ark, And knew not until the flood came, and took them all away; so shall also the coming of the Son of man be (Matthew 24:37-39).

But there are further and more ominous conditions which are listed in Scripture describing the times of Noah. These conditions, which once led directly to the Flood upon "the world that was", are increasingly becoming prevalent in our own time, and portend the final divine judgment upon this world.

6) Violence Covered the Earth.

The days of Noah were characterized by violence. The proud boasting in the first recorded song in the Bible, that of Lamech (from Cain's line) is a snapshot of the in-your-face attitude of those dark times.

If God would avenge Cain with some punishment which extends beyond physical death, Lamech himself would extract seventy times as much vengeance, and for far less of a personal offense, upon any who so much as slighted him!

In Lamech's self-glorification, and perhaps even self-deification, we see an example of the cause of the overflowing violence. Having turned their backs upon the worship and acknowledgment of "Most High", the earth swarmed with hundreds of thousands with the same mindset as Lamech; self-made heroes, lovers of themselves, boasters, heady, high-minded ones, ever ready to avenge themselves at the slightest provocation.

Is this not the apostolic description of the day we live in today?

> This know also, that in the last days perilous times shall come. For men shall be lovers of their own selves, covetous, boasters, proud, blasphemers, disobedient to parents, unthankful, unholy, Without natural affection, trucebreakers, false accusers, incontinent, fierce, despisers of those that are good, Traitors, heady, highminded, lovers of pleasures more than lovers of God (2 Timothy 3:1-4).

Lamech's song could easily pass for the "Rap" music, which millions fill their souls with today, and who dress and emulate the "Rappers" violent, aggressive, self-absorbed lifestyles. These modern Lamechs sell millions of CDs and pornographic DVDs to young people, containing songs which glorify rape, theft, race war, murder, fornication and adultery.

Racial inequality is constantly emphasized by parasitical "Civil Rights" leaders who demagogue their own people, keeping them resentful, poor and dependent upon the government, with a constant, ready excuse for their manifest failure. It couldn't possibly be the breakdown of the family, the almost complete absence of fathers in the home, and the abandonment of any trace of Judeo-Christian morality that is afflicting the "community". It has to be the all-purpose excuse "racism"!

With forty plus years of such resentment being stoked, it is no wonder that the inner cities of America have become virtual war zones of random violence and murder. Games such as "Knock Out King", in which an unsuspecting passer-by is literally punched in the face without warning, all the while being filmed on cell phone, to be posted on YouTube, have become alarmingly popular pastimes for the resentful and unemployable youth of our inner cities. So also are the violent flash mobs, which converge on strangers, men, women and children, robbing and beating people just because they happen to be of a different race.

As our Western democracies veer ever farther left, the politicians have stoked up the potential for violence and resentment, by constantly advocating a sense of entitlement to other people's property, as class envy is increasingly codified into law by the ever-growing masses of "low information voters". Thus violence is covering the earth, as in the days of Noah.

Furthermore, the resurgence of the most violent and intolerant religion the world has ever seen, Islam, is covering the earth with violence also. Since the shocking 9-11 attack there have been 20,000 major Islamic terror attacks on the civilized world. Billions of dollars have had to be expended on security measures and there is nowhere on earth that has escaped the scourge of the Islamic bloodlust.

The LORD of history has seen fit to orchestrate the modern world's dependence on oil. It so happens that the cheapest, and easiest to extract pure crude oil was discovered under the sands of the very birthplace of the strictest Islamic sect, the Wahhabis of Arabia. And it's a fact that the house of Saud has long been the guardians of this vicious religion.

The nations of the Western world have prostituted their highest ideals to appease the Saudis, looking the other way as they have used their oil wealth to bankroll terrorism, suppress human rights, and metastasize their peculiarly violent brand of Islam around the world, radicalizing Muslims across the globe.

Europe has even agreed to accept the immigration of the excess of the teeming Arabian populations, blanketing the civilized world with hostile and potentially violent masses who hate everything their host countries stand for. It seems, that since the European nations didn't want the Jews, God has sent them instead the Muslims as a judgment.

A terrible storm is about to break as the clouds of the last judgment approach. Now would be a good time for the fearful to hear the glad words of the prophet Joel, that in the midst of the coming storm, *"Whosoever would call upon the name of the Lord will be saved".*

<> <> <>

And God saw that the wickedness of man was great in the earth, and that every imagination of the thoughts of his heart was only evil continually. And it repented the Lord that he had made man on the earth, and it grieved him at his heart (Genesis 6:5-6).

WE HAVE BEEN LOOKING at the universal conditions that led directly to the Flood in the "days of Noah", because Jesus told us that this same state of affairs will be duplicated in some way at the time of the Parousia, and the final judgment of this world. *"As in the days of Noah, so shall the coming of the Son of Man be"* at the end of this age, according to the Savior.

We have thus far considered six of the stated conditions: 1) A population explosion, 2) Rapid progress in technology, science and the arts, 3) A complete disregard for the original ideal of marriage, 4) the blurring of the distinction between the people of God and the world, 5) the rejection of a line of preachers of righteousness and judgment, and finally in the last section we discussed 6) violence covering the earth.

We come to another startlingly modern sign of the days of Noah—the fact that in those days God said,

7) The thoughts and imaginations of men's hearts were only evil continually.

Imagination is a God-given attribute, part of the image of God with which we were created. We men and women can conceptualize and picture in our minds almost limitless possibilities. By imagination we are able to create, plan, foresee, and visualize. We can dream and fantasize in our hearts for both good and evil purposes.

But Jesus warned us that because of the Fall of man and the subsequent corruption of our nature, the things which proceed from the heart, are what defile us.

> And he said, That which cometh out of the man, that defileth the man. For from within, out of the heart of men, proceed evil thoughts, adulteries, fornications, murders, Thefts, covetousness, wickedness, deceit, lasciviousness, an evil eye, blasphemy, pride, foolishness: All these evil things come from within, and defile the man (Mark 7:20-23).

The human heart has become an "idol factory" according to one of the reformers, for fallen men are constantly devising images unworthy of God or of those bearing the likeness of God. Those self-conceived images, formed by the deceitful lusts of the heart, shape and guide men, away from God, and after their fallen desires.

People tend to follow their most cherished inner concept, the image of what they love, the ideal that they regard as the most beautiful, whether it be the image of "world peace", utopia, the vision of Humanism, Islam or Communism. (In fact all "isms" are actually man-made idols, rivals to God and His plan for the world). This is why it is so important to love and seek the "only true God and Jesus Christ whom He has sent".

When there is enough peace, prosperity and leisure, men tend to have more time to devote to the development of their imaginations, and images. In the days of Noah and even in the days of Lot, Jesus tells us that people were

> And as it was in the days of Noe, so shall it be also in the days of the Son of man. They did eat, they drank, they married wives, they were given in marriage, until the day that Noah entered into the ark, and the flood came, and destroyed them all. Likewise also as it was in the days of Lot; they did eat, they drank, they bought, they sold, they planted, they builded (Luke 17:26-28).

The people of Noah's day had the time to indulge in imagination. Obviously they weren't living "hand to mouth"; there was a vibrant economy, and people got into trade, food, entertainment, the arts, drink, and relationships. None of these things is evil in itself, but note the absence of God in their actions and thoughts. When left to themselves, the imaginations of men tend towards evil.

What we are living in now is a revolution of the indulgence of human imagination. Our technology facilitates it. Most people who have ever lived could not have conceived of radio, let alone television! Think of what the television revolution has done to the imaginations of modern man. People can get lost in a soap opera or a sitcom, they can become fascinated by a movie or documentary.

Even more so than radio and television is the explosion of technology that allows one to privately screen any movie he wants, anytime he wants. Put the "buds" in his ears, tune everyone else out, and immerse oneself in story after story, meditating the contrived, special effected imaginations of Hollywood directors and screen writers for hours without interruption.

Rarely is the question asked, "What becomes of the soul which has immersed him or herself into the imaginations of degenerates such as Spike Lee, Quenton Tarantino, or even Mel Gibson?" Thousands of titles of blood-soaked, gratuitously violent, blasphemous, sexually provocative films are constantly on call for PC users, who no longer need to think, but can at will enter into other worlds for hours at a time.

Perhaps more ominous are the computer games which millions of people have plunged their minds, hearts, affections and hours of time into. One doesn't merely play board games, such as Chess or Stratego with a friend anymore. Such were the leisure pursuits of the past. Now, with the flip of a switch, one enters through imagination, into the killing fields of World War 2 or into a bizarre fantasy world of witches, warlocks, dragons, spells and curses, or into a football arena, a boxing ring, or a coliseum.

Many of the more sensationally violent crimes, such as the recent school or theater shootings which have stunned and rocked us, have been committed by mentally ill loners, often on prescription medication, and often hopelessly addicted to video games, many of which consist of the vicarious experience of going from room to room, and shooting at close range the virtual enemies who pop out at them.

Through our modern technology, millions have entered completely into evil imaginations. They now have the tools to escape from the burden of any painful contemplation, and to elude conviction from an uneasy conscience that all is not well.

Through their iTunes lists, or selection of movies or hours of video games, such thoughts don't even stand a chance of entering their minds. They have already preprogrammed their thoughts, and are in danger of putting themselves out of reach of recovery.

What is it that many of these millions have fixed their minds on? Go walk through a video game store, and you will see shelf after shelf of evil. The occult, witchcraft, grand theft larceny games, where one can role play at being a pimp, a gangster, a pirate, or whatever evil you can "imagine". It is all available, and widely used.

Have you seen what is popular on iTunes? All of the soul-destroying trash from the sixties and seventies is now regarded as quaint, mainstream music. The Beatles, Led Zeppelin, Styx, indeed all of the drug-promoting, occult-based "rock and roll" that churches once warned about and exposed is now as popular as ever thanks to the new technology.

We are rapidly approaching the frightening point referred to in Genesis, where *"men's hearts are continually set on evil"*. At least before this shift in technology in the field of entertainment, it would have been impossible to constantly be distracted and amused by fast moving, high quality images. People had to think.

But we have created a highly entertaining, completely immersing world of constantly shifting images, many of which draw their inspiration from the occult, or various violent scenarios, wherein it could truly be said that of a good many, *"the imaginations of men's hearts became continually evil"*.

> And it came to pass, when men began to multiply on the face of the earth, and daughters were born unto them, That the sons of God saw the daughters of men that they were fair; and they took them wives of all which they chose. And the Lord said, My spirit shall not always strive with man, for that he also is flesh: yet his days shall be an hundred and twenty years (Genesis 6:1-3).

The signs of the day of Noah that we have discussed earlier—the population explosion, rapid progress in science, technology and the arts, the complete disregard for the primal law of marriage, the blurring of distinction between the lines of the godly and the godless, as well as the rejection of the preaching of judgment and repentance by Seth, Enoch, Methuselah and Lamech, and the increasing phenomenon of universal violence—had come to a head.

God had allowed conditions on earth to be such that people lived hundreds of years on earth. But increasingly, those years were almost universally lived out in a state of God-rejection, evil practices, and as a society, an incredible, exponentially growing accumulation of evil. The dark "wisdom" of people who lived for hundreds of years was passed on to each generation, until men and women became hardened beyond any recovery.

But Genesis 6 records a new stage in the progress of evil, something so terrible it is almost impossible to contemplate. Sinful humanity, schooled in dark wisdom, broke through the barrier to communion between fallen angels and God-estranged humanity.

We are told that the *"Sons of God saw the daughters of men that they were fair, and took of them wives".*

The phrase, the "Sons of God" is a reference to angels, fallen or otherwise, as recorded here in Job, which is believed to be the oldest book of the Bible.

> Now there was a day when the sons of God came to present themselves before the Lord, and Satan came also among them. And the Lord said unto Satan, Whence comest thou? Then Satan answered the Lord, and said, From going to and fro in the earth, and from walking up and down in it (Job 1:6-7).

It was at the mention of this dark and mysterious development among men, that the Most High decreed a further limitation upon human life.

> **And the Lord said, My spirit shall not always strive with man, for that he also is flesh: yet his days shall be an hundred and twenty years.**

There would no longer be hundreds of years of God-rejection and accumulation of the experience and "wisdom" of evil. At best, man would be allowed 120 years to respond to the conviction and internal strivings of his Creator.

The Lord's apostles Jude and Peter both refer to this horrifying state of affairs.

> And the angels which **kept not their first estate,** but left their own habitation, he hath reserved

in everlasting chains under darkness unto the judgment of the great day. Even as Sodom and Gomorrha, and the cities about them in like manner, giving themselves over to fornication, and **going after strange flesh**, are set forth for an example, suffering the vengeance of eternal fire (Jude 6-7).

Jude likens the angels which left their own God-assigned state, to Sodomites who go "after strange flesh". Both sins consist of the unnatural joining of that which God separates, and both bring violent and everlasting punishment.

Peter also referenced this sin, linking it to Noah, the Flood and Sodom and Gomorrah.

For if God spared not the **angels that sinned**, but cast them down to hell, and delivered them into chains of darkness, to be reserved unto judgment; And spared not the old world, but saved Noah the eighth person, a preacher of righteousness, bringing in the flood upon the world of the ungodly; And **turning the cities of Sodom and Gomorrha into ashes** condemned them with an overthrow, making them an ensample unto those that after should live ungodly (2 Peter 2:4-6).

Both apostles emphasize the immediacy and ferocity of the divine judgment which fell upon these angels and those who participated with them. The Flood, and the fact that those very angels are presently in chains in a hellish prison awaiting their time of judgment with the rest of the fallen angels, testified to the seriousness of this sin.

But consider our day also, which is rapidly proving to be "as in the days of Noah and Lot". How many Hollywood movies have had as their theme the intercourse, spiritual and otherwise, of angels and men?

Popular abominations such as "The City of Angels" starring Nicholas Cage, have as their theme romantic interplay between an angel of God, (who leaves his first estate because he falls in love with one of the fair daughters of men, sacrificing his own immortality), could have been lifted right off of the pages of Genesis.[17]

These movies are popular because they reflect aspirations among people for such things; angel movies, super hero movies, UFO and alien movies all reflect the same aspiration for communion with beings above and beyond humanity, but definitely not with the God of the Bible on the terms of Calvary. This is the very sin that brought the Flood which wiped out the whole world, except the eight people who were saved.

<> <> <>

And it came to pass, when men began to multiply on the face of the earth, and daughters were born unto them, That the sons of God saw the daughters of men that they were fair; and they took them wives of all which they chose. And the Lord said, My spirit shall not always strive with man, for that he also is flesh: yet his days shall be an hundred and twenty years. There were giants in the earth in those days; and also after that, when the sons of God came in unto the daughters of men, and they bare children to them, the same became mighty men which were of old, men of renown. And God saw that the wickedness of man was great in the earth, and that every imagination of the thoughts of his heart was only evil continually. And it repented the Lord that he had made man on the earth, and it grieved him at his heart (Genesis 6:1-6).

WE HAVE ALREADY DISCUSSED the manifold conditions which led up to the Flood; the population explosion, rapid increase in technology, agriculture and the arts with a view to mitigating the curse without repentance, the disregard for the primal laws of marriage, the confusion of sexual roles, the exponential increase in violence, the eradication of distinction between the godly and the ungodly, and the overall rejection of the prophetic warning.

Finally, sinful humanity arrived at a new stage in the progress of evil, for some among them, dared breach the divine barrier to interaction between fallen angel and man. This developed to the point of actual union between the "daughters of men" and the fallen angelic "Sons of God", the "angels who kept not their first estate" as the Lord's apostles told us.

Scripture tells us the unthinkable, that out of the union of humans and fallen angels came the "giants", literally the *nephilim*, the "fallen ones". This rebellious hybridization of the human race, mixing men and angels (I have no idea how this was possible, but Scripture teaches this), is literally the final sin that brought the Flood.

These "mighty ones", the "men of renown" were not necessarily "giants" in the sense of size. Some of them may have been "gigantic" indeed, as were Goliath and his brothers centuries later. But the idea is that this hybridized humanity, these "fallen ones" were remarkable for power and intelligence as well as stature. They were prodigies or heroes.

There are many who believe that figures such as the Greek and Roman gods Hercules, (half man and half god), or the Titans ,"sons of heaven and earth" came from the distant human memory of these pre-Flood monsters. They were famous for their exploits, feats of strength or perhaps of intelligence. But they were evil.

In our own day, the fascination of the young with super

heroes is an ominous portent. Usually the super heroes are said to be "good". They fight for "justice". But what are we to make of the new gay super hero, or of "Superman" a savior son sent to earth, found in a "barn" and raised by adoptive parents.

In the trailer for the movie, "Superman", Marlon Brando's voice narrates for Superman's father, Jor-El, from outer space, commissioning his son to come into the world to allow humanity to reach its full human potential.

> Even though you've been raised as a human being you're not one of them. They can be a great people, Kal-El. They wish to be. They only lack the light to show the way. For this reason above all, their capacity for good, I sent them you . . . my only son.

Fallen humanity yearns for a humanistic salvation brought about by humanistic "saviors", men of powers, famous for their exploits, who make no moral demands, and show no weakness, nor do they turn us back in humility to our Creator.

Whether it be the fascination with super heroes, or the fantasy world, or apparitions of the Virgin Mary, or channeled Spirits, the Mahdi, visualization, there is something for everyone now, for we are again in the days of Noah.

The spiritual world has broken through to communication with the sons and daughters of men. Several decades of massive rejection of the Judeo-Christian message, with the vacuum filled by an influx of Eastern Religions, the occult, drug usage, Transcendental Meditation, Islam, and New Age spirituality has opened the "door of consciousness" to the invasion of evil spirits and the frightening deception they bring upon the world.

<> <> <>

And the Lord said, I will destroy man whom I have created from the face of the earth; both man, and beast, and the creeping thing, and the fowls of the air; for it repenteth me that I have made them. But Noah found grace in the eyes of the Lord. These are the generations of Noah: Noah was a just man and perfect in his generations, and Noah walked with God. And Noah begat three sons, Shem, Ham, and Japheth. The earth also was corrupt before God, and the earth was filled with violence. And God looked upon the earth, and, behold, it was corrupt; for all flesh had corrupted his way upon the earth. And God said unto Noah, The end of all flesh is come before me; for the earth is filled with violence through them; and, behold, I will destroy them with the earth (Genesis 6:7-13).

THE WORLD OF NOAH'S day was on the verge of total destruction, though few knew it. The godlessness and the resulting violence, perversion, rampant distortion of sexuality, and constant indulgence in the imagination of evil was almost entirely universal. Man, who had been made in the image of God, had willfully become a sick, and twisted parody of that image.

How corrupt and evil had man become? Scripture literally quotes God saying, **"It hurts me to the heart, that I have made man"**.

Yet, the apostle Peter tells us, *"the longsuffering of God is salvation"*. God waited for centuries, to save any who would turn to Him. The Sethite line, and particularly Enoch, Methuselah and Lamech all bore witness to sinners of the coming judgment.

The Lord's apostle Peter tells us, that "The Lord is not

slack, concerning his promises as some men count slackness, but is not willing that any should perish, but that all should come to repentance".

But even in judgment, God remembers mercy, for we are told that, *"Noah found grace in the eyes of the Lord".*

In this first mention of grace in Scripture, we see the portrait of the salvation of everyman, for in a sense all of us are like Noah.

- **Noah didn't deserve to be saved.** Grace is defined as the undeserved favor of God. When God says Noah found grace, He is saying by inference, that Noah received something from God that he didn't deserve, and that he couldn't earn or merit. That something is called *"righteousness"* or *"right standing with God".*

  True, Noah is also said to be a *"a just man and perfect in his generations, and Noah walked with God",* but the rest of Scripture teaches us that the "justness" Noah possessed was a gift of God, given to those who believe God, and who walk with God as a consequence of God's continual justification.

  In a doomed world of sinners given completely over to their depraved lusts, God chose one man and his family, giving them the gift of righteousness. Noah believed God, and right standing with God was imputed to him. Noah walked with God in faith and humble worship, in a world that had spurned and rejected God.

- **All of us live in a doomed world.** Ours is a world under judgment as Noah's was. The sentence has been passed and it is only a matter of time before the infinitely righteous and holy Judge of all of the earth executes the sentence upon the world of the ungodly. The prophet Isaiah bears witness to this.

> Behold, the Lord maketh the earth empty, and
> maketh it waste, and turneth it upside down, and
> scattereth abroad the inhabitants thereof . . . The
> land shall be utterly emptied, and utterly spoiled:
> for the Lord hath spoken this word. The earth
> mourneth and fadeth away, the world languisheth
> and fadeth away, the haughty people of the earth
> do languish. The earth also is defiled under the
> inhabitants thereof; because they have trans-
> gressed the laws, changed the ordinance, broken
> the everlasting covenant (Isaiah 24:1-4.)

The apostle Paul also warns us of the coming day of divine examination.

> But after thy hardness and impenitent heart trea-
> surest up unto thyself wrath against the day of
> wrath and revelation of the righteous judgment of
> God; Who will render to every man according to
> his deeds (Romans 2:5-6).

God's attitude towards this world is uncompromising.
It is slated for destruction. There is no way that the church
is going to be able to "make the world a better place". The
world has already been judged. God is now calling people to
come out of this world.

- **God has shown us something also.** God showed Noah
  what was coming, something that the rest of the world
  had willfully ignored until they rendered themselves
  oblivious to it. God has shown His people in our day also
  that the dreaded Day of Judgment is coming. God's people know something that the rest of the world either is
  ignorant of, or in denial about.

In fact the least member of any true church, knows more
about the problems of the world, and the outcome of them,
than all of the Kings of the earth, the pundits, scholars and
think tanks combined!

- **Grace moves us to action.** Noah was shown something from God about the judgment that was coming on the ungodly world, and what to do about it. Noah didn't hesitate. He responded to the grace of God, in the fear of God. We, too, have been shown something about the coming of the Lord and the just judgment coming on the world. This revelation is supposed to drive us in humble faith and repentance to Jesus Christ, the new and living ark God has prepared.

> By faith Noah, being warned of God of things not seen as yet, moved with fear, prepared an ark to the saving of his house; by the which he condemned the world, and became heir of the righteousness which is by faith (Hebrews 11:7).

> Now when they heard this, they were pricked in their heart, and said unto Peter and to the rest of the apostles, **Men and brethren, what shall we do?** Then Peter said unto them, Repent, and be baptized every one of you in the name of Jesus Christ for the remission of sins, and ye shall receive the gift of the Holy Ghost. For the promise is unto you, and to your children, and to all that are afar off, even as many as the Lord our God shall call. And with many other words did he testify and exhort, saying, **Save yourselves from this untoward generation** (Acts 2:37-40).

- **Noah's action condemned the world.** It took Noah 120 years to build the ark. What a spectacle it must have been! But the erection of this massive structure was a daily warning and condemnation of the world, a testament that it was doomed and under wrath.

This is why there has always been persecution against the church by the world. Somehow or another, the world perceives that it is being condemned by Christians, especially by the sacrament of adult baptism. They may not know the doctrine, but they correctly sense that a valid baptism is crossing a watery line from one world to another, and announcing the end of the old world.

Peter tells us that every Christian baptism does just that. Every time a person goes under the water in the name of Jesus Christ, they are proclaiming that this world is under judgment, and that it won't last long, which is why they are leaving it to enter into Christ.

> For Christ also hath once suffered for sins, the just for the unjust, that he might bring us to God, being put to death in the flesh, but quickened by the Spirit: By which also he went and preached unto the spirits in prison; Which sometime were disobedient, when once the longsuffering of God waited in the days of Noah, while the ark was a preparing, wherein few, that is, eight souls were saved by water. The like figure whereunto even baptism doth also now save us (not the putting away of the filth of the flesh, but the answer of a good conscience toward God,) by the resurrection of Jesus Christ (1 Peter 3:18-21).

<> <> <>

And God looked upon the earth, and, behold, it was corrupt; for all flesh had corrupted his way upon the earth. And God said unto Noah, The end of all flesh is come before me; for the earth is filled with violence through them; and, behold, I will destroy them with the earth. Make thee an ark of gopher wood; rooms shalt thou make in the ark, and shalt pitch it within and without with pitch. And this is the fashion which thou shalt make it of: The length of the ark shall be three hundred cubits, the breadth of it fifty cubits, and the height of it thirty cubits. A window shalt thou make to the ark, and in a cubit shalt thou finish it above; and the door of the ark shalt thou set in the side thereof; with lower, second, and third stories shalt thou make it. And, behold, I, even I, do bring a flood of waters upon the earth, to destroy all flesh, wherein is the breath of life, from under heaven; and every thing that is in the earth shall die (Genesis 6:12-17).

GOD HAD "LOOKED AT the earth". That is, He examined it for judgment, seeing the utter corruption and violence. The sentence was passed, the verdict was rendered, and His attitude towards it was uncompromising; the earth, and all upon it who had received the "breath of life" were slated for destruction.

There would be no "salvaging" of the earth, even as there can be no "improving" of our current world today. We will not be able ever to "make this world a better place". God has judged it. The sentence has been passed. All that remains is the final execution of the sentence.

Our Savior proclaimed as He rode into Jerusalem for His final week on earth leading up to Calvary, *"Now is the judgment of this world, now is the prince of this world cast down."* The world is under judgment and God's view of it is uncompromising. It is doomed to utter destruction, along with Satan, the proud "prince of this world" and all who will follow him to perdition.

The only question in the day of Noah, as well as in our day, is, "Has God provided a way of escape for any of us?" Is there a way out?

The answer given in Noah's day was the ark, which God

commanded to be built for those who had "found grace with God", Noah and his family. The very God who had purposed to absolutely "judge the world in righteousness", also ordained a refuge from the wrath of God.

We, too, who live in the last days, a time Jesus described as being "as in the days of Noah", have been given a way out of the coming storm of judgment that is already gathering for this wicked, God-rejecting, doomed world. Our Ark isn't a boat. He is a person, the Lord Jesus Christ, the friend of sinners, and the only refuge from the wrath of God.

The ark of Noah, is a type of Christ, as partially seen in these aspects—

- The ark was the provision of God. Its pattern and mandate came from God. God showed Noah his need of salvation, and gave him the pattern to erect it.

- In a similar way, God has shown us who are Christians something. He has revealed by His Spirit that this world is under judgment and we likewise are doomed with it, to perdition. And He has revealed Jesus Christ, crucified and raised from the dead as the place of refuge.

- Gopher wood, the material for the ark, reminds us that the means of our salvation likewise comes by the tree. "He bore our sins upon the tree that we should die to sin and live to righteousness and by His stripes we are healed".

- God Himself called Noah to come into the ark. The author Pink notes that this is the first use of the word "come" in Scripture.

Observe that the Lord does not say "*Go* into the ark," but "Come." "Go" would have been a command, "Come"

was a gracious invitation; "Go" would have implied that the Lord was bidding Noah *depart* from Him, "Come" intimated that in the ark the Lord would be present with him. Is it not the same thought as we have in the Gospel—"Come *unto Me* and I will give you rest!"[18]

- The Ark had only one door. There is only one way to be saved, and only one entrance into the Kingdom of God. Jesus Himself is the door of salvation. Jesus said, *"I am the way, the truth, and the light, and no man comes to the Father, but by Me".* The door of the ark was placed "in the side of it", according to the divine pattern. Jesus was pierced in the side and revealed the opening to Thomas, assuring him that the way of salvation had been opened.

- The ark had one window, one source of light, placed on the roof. The light was above them. They were to "look up" to God for illumination.

- The "pitch " which covered gopher wood of the ark, making it watertight and secure, is called in the Hebrew, **kepher.** This is the same word which is translated many other places in the Old Testament, "to cover" or "to make atonement". Because we have been covered over, with Jesus' perfect righteousness, God's judgment fell upon Jesus. He covered us. He took our place as a substitute for us and bore the storm of the wrath of God!

The ark, ordained of God like the Messiah Jesus whom it points to, is nothing less than a refuge from the wrath of God. Oh that men would flee into Him before it is too late!

9

The Open Door of the Ark

And the Lord said unto Noah, Come thou and all thy
house into the ark; for thee have I seen righteous
before me in this generation. Of every clean beast
thou shalt take to thee by sevens, the male and his
female: and of beasts that are not clean by two,
the male and his female. Of fowls also of the air
by sevens, the male and the female; to keep seed
alive upon the face of all the earth. For yet seven
days, and I will cause it to rain upon the earth forty
days and forty nights; and every living substance
that I have made will I destroy from off the face of
the earth. And Noah did according unto all that
the Lord commanded him (Genesis 7:1-5).

ENOCH, LAMECH, METHUSELAH AND Noah, and no doubt many
others over the centuries, had long warned of the day of
God's wrath upon the earth. Perhaps at the beginning they
preached to a receptive audience, but by the time of the
events of Genesis chapter 7 the warnings fell on deaf ears.

The society of Noah's day was completely depraved; it
was violent, inclined towards evil, hateful of any trace of
goodness, constantly developing evil imaginations, and ex-

cept for eight souls to whom God had granted grace, completely God-rejecting.

The final progression of human evil was achieved when men openly initiated intimate contact with fallen beings. Thus did angels and men alike transgress the divine boundary, bringing upon the angels that sinned a premature sentence to confinement; and upon the world of men, a flood of near total destruction.

As the apostle Peter warned,

> For if God spared not the angels that sinned, but cast them down to hell, and delivered them into chains of darkness, to be reserved unto judgment; And spared not the old world, but saved Noah the eighth person, a preacher of righteousness, bringing in the flood upon the world of the ungodly (2 Peter 2:4-5).

The ark had been prepared, the clean and unclean animals were drawn in, and the door of the ark was opened, as Noah and his family went about their final preparations and warnings.

It is interesting to note that the call to Noah and his family was not to "go into the ark", but to "come into the ark". God was in the ark, calling from within to Noah. Centuries later, the Messiah of God, who is also a refuge from the coming wrath of God, called out in a similar fashion to whosoever would hear.

> Come unto me, all ye that labour and are heavy laden, and I will give you rest. Take my yoke upon you, and learn of me; for I am meek and lowly in heart: and ye shall find rest unto your souls. For my yoke is easy, and my burden is light (Matthew 11:28-30).

God was going to wipe out all human life, except for

those eight. Indeed the Lord was preparing to extinguish all life of any kind—fowl, mammal, reptile, in short everything that He had made that breathes air. Every man, woman and child was soon to experience the utter wrath of the Holy God whom they had long spurned and ignored.

They had in times past, no doubt, been exposed to the preaching of judgment, and perhaps in various cases they had been moved by it. Certainly the time span since Creation had included two overlapping lives who would have been profound witnesses to the reality and judgment of God. For the first 930 years, the world had Adam among them as a witness.

Methuselah, the son of Enoch, also was a living witness, whose life overlapped Adam's, to span the entire pre-Flood era. His name itself was a prophecy, *"when he dies, it comes"*, or *"his death shall bring . . ."*. The world that once was, would last as long as Methuselah. The very year he died, the Flood came.

The fact that Methuselah lived longer than any other human being is also a witness to another fact. It tells us that "the Lord is not slack concerning His promise (of judgment) as some count slackness, but is longsuffering toward us, not wishing for any to perish, but for all to come to repentance"!

The door to the ark stood open, although daily it seemed less relevant, less compelling and necessary to the world as it rushed towards the precipice of deeper sin , reprobation, and the coming judgment. People became oblivious to the call to repentance. Consciences died and hearts hardened, as the pace of life advanced, with its exotic foods, drink, marriages, building projects, entertainments, and the enticing "new spirituality" introduced to the world by the "fallen ones".

It seemed that in spite of the obvious problems (violence), man was progressing in every other way without God!

Jesus warned that at the time of His return the same delusion would prevail.

> But as the days of Noah were, so shall also the coming of the Son of man be. For as in the days that were before the flood they were eating and drinking, marrying and giving in marriage, until the day that Noe entered into the ark, And knew not until the flood came, and took them all away; so shall also the coming of the Son of man be (Matthew 24:37-39).

As the voices of Enoch, Lamech, Methuselah and even Noah began to fade out of public awareness, the gloomy clouds of divine vengeance began to form and roil, but the party just went on without notice.

<> <> <>

In the selfsame day entered Noah, and Shem, and Ham, and Japheth, the sons of Noah, and Noah's wife, and the three wives of his sons with them, into the ark; They, and every beast after his kind, and all the cattle after their kind, and every creeping thing that creepeth upon the earth after his kind, and every fowl after his kind, every bird of every sort. And they went in unto Noah into the ark, two and two of all flesh, wherein is the breath of life. And they that went in, went in male and female of all flesh, as God had commanded him: and **the Lord shut him in** *(Genesis 7:13-16).*

SEVEN DAYS BEFORE THE long promised, yet long-delayed wrath of God was poured out upon the earth, the Lord called Noah into the ark, along with the clean and unclean animals and birds and beasts which God had assembled. They waited there in the ark for one week, no doubt to allow any other people from the "world that was" to escape.

The door remained open for one final week. Whosoever would but heed the call of Noah and his renowned fathers, Enoch, Methuselah and Lamech, could yet be saved. But by the time of the last week the people were utterly oblivious. Jesus said of them that it was business as usual for them *". . . until the day Noah entered into the ark, they knew not until the flood came and took them all away" (Matthew 24:39).*

After seven days, God Himself closed the door.

What is the significance in Scripture of the open or closed door? As long as the door is open, there remains a chance for men to be saved from the coming wrath. But there does come a time when God closes the door.

We are told in the another story of judgment and escape, that as righteous Lot was vexed by the wickedness of Sodom and Gomorrah, the perverted "men of the city" compassed the house, gathering at Lot's door.

> And Lot went out at the door unto them, and shut the door after him, And said, I pray you, brethren, do not so wickedly. Behold now, I have two daughters which have not known man; let me, I pray you, bring them out unto you, and do ye to them as is good in your eyes: only unto these men do nothing; for therefore came they under the shadow of my roof. And they said, Stand back. And they said again, This one fellow came in to sojourn, and he will needs be a judge: now will we deal worse with thee, than with them. And they pressed sore upon the man, even Lot, and came near to break the door. But the men put forth their hand, and pulled Lot into the house to them, and shut to the door. And they smote the men that were at the door of the house with blindness, both small and great: so that they wearied themselves to find the door (Genesis 19:6-11).

Notice that Lot himself tried to shut the door on the menacing revelers of Sodom, but they nearly broke the door down in order to ravage Lot's angelic guests. Lot wasn't able to shut the door, for God alone can open or shut the ultimate doors. It was only when God's angels pulled Lot into the house and shut Lot's door, that the door was effectively shut.

Once the door was shut, those outside were blinded and unable to so much as find the door. (Try to imagine being driven by so great a lust that even when blinded by angels, they sought to get in and ravage the guests!).

Jesus used the same metaphor when He warned the presumptuous who imagine that they are already saved by virtue of being close to Jesus, or perhaps having taken communion, or hearing Christian teaching, without ever having been broken under conviction and truly calling upon the name of the Lord.

> When once the master of the house is risen up, and **hath shut to the door**, and ye begin to stand without, and to knock at the door, saying, Lord, Lord, open unto us; and he shall answer and say unto you, I know you not whence ye are: Then shall ye begin to say, We have eaten and drunk in thy presence, and thou hast taught in our streets; But he shall say, I tell you, I know you not whence ye are; depart from me, all ye workers of iniquity. There shall be weeping and gnashing of teeth, when ye shall see Abraham, and Isaac, and Jacob, and all the prophets, in the kingdom of God, and you yourselves thrust out (Luke 13:25-28).

Does not our Lord refer to Himself as "the door"? He alone, to whom the ark of Noah only pointed, is the way to the heavenly Father. He is the only true refuge from the coming storm of God's wrath.

Then said Jesus unto them again, Verily, verily, I say unto you, I am the door of the sheep. All that ever came before me are thieves and robbers: but the sheep did not hear them. I am the door: by me if any man enter in, he shall be saved, and shall go in and out, and find pasture (John 10:7-9).

For the time being the door is open, but the hour is late. Soon the Master will rise and shut the door, and whoever is in will remain in, but those who are out will be stuck, outside the door. Few in Noah's day realized the significance of the obscure little family moving into the huge wooden structure they had been working on for 120 years. As the assortment of animals began to climb aboard the structure, perhaps some wondered . . . but not for long.

There were too many other amusements, distractions, fine foods and entertainments going on for them to think too deeply about the eccentric family with its menagerie of animals, clambering aboard the pitch-covered building. After seven days of settling and waiting within the ark, the door was shut and the raindrops began to fall.

<> <> <>

And the flood was forty days upon the earth; and the waters increased, and bare up the ark, and it was lift up above the earth. And the waters prevailed, and were increased greatly upon the earth; and the ark went upon the face of the waters. And the waters prevailed exceedingly upon the earth; and all the high hills, that were under the whole heaven, were covered. Fifteen cubits upward did the waters prevail; and the mountains were covered. And all flesh died that moved upon the earth, both of fowl, and of cattle, and of beast, and of every creeping thing that creepeth upon the earth, and every

> *man: All in whose nostrils was the breath of life, of*
> *all that was in the dry land, died. And every living*
> *substance was destroyed which was upon the face of*
> *the ground, both man, and cattle, and the creeping*
> *things, and the fowl of the heaven; and they were*
> *destroyed from the earth: and Noah only remained*
> *alive, and they that were with him in the ark. And*
> *the waters prevailed upon the earth an hundred*
> *and fifty days (Genesis 7:17-24).*

FOR FORTY DAYS AND nights, water poured down upon the earth from the rent liquid canopy that God had set in the heavens. Water also shot up out of the earth in violent torrents from the massive underground storehouses of water, set in place at Creation. By the time the deluge had ceased, the tips of the highest mountains on earth were twenty-two feet under water.

All life, men, women, children, and any animal or bird life which once drew breath, were drowned. Ancient cities, which dated back to Cain's original city, Enoch, were wiped out, buried under tons of mud and debris from the shifting land masses. Entire forests were instantly buried under tons of mud; trees, shrubs, beasts, birds, were all thrown into the cataclysmic heaps we find today in the "fossil record".

But for 150 days none of that would have been visible. Had Noah been able to get a glimpse outside through the one window on the ark, he would have seen nothing but the waves of water in every direction. The entire old world was erased by the water. It perished in the water, as Peter described it—

> Whereby the world that then was, being overflowed with water, perished (2 Peter 3:9).

The water, sent by God, served several distinct purposes which are worth noting. What did the water do?

- **The water was an instrument of divine wrath.** It killed everything and everybody of the *"world that then was"*. God is a Holy God. He hates sin and evil, and when it became evident that the human race was reprobating itself, and after allowing a very long time for repentance, God judged the world, putting it to death in the deluge.

- **The water was a burial of that which was dead.** What do we do with a corpse? We bury it. The water served as a burial of that which was dead. From the dust came the "world that then was"; to the dust it returned, via the water.

- **The water served as a means of salvation and separation.** The same water which buried the old world, lifted Noah and his family above and out of it. The Flood, we are told, *"bore up the ark, it was lifted up above the earth"*. Peter links the Flood of Noah to believers' baptism, teaching,

> For Christ also hath once suffered for sins, the just for the unjust, that he might bring us to God, being put to death in the flesh, but quickened by the Spirit: By which also he went and preached unto the spirits in prison; Which sometime were disobedient, when once the longsuffering of God waited in the days of Noah, while the ark was a preparing, wherein few, that is, **eight souls were saved by water.** The like figure whereunto even baptism doth also now save us (not the putting away of the filth of the flesh, but the answer of a good conscience toward God,) by the resurrection of Jesus Christ (1 Peter 3:18-20).

Note the phrase "eight souls were saved by water". The same water that condemned the world, lifted up the ark, separating it from the world it had fled, removing Noah and his family from the mudslides and other cataclysmic events that fell upon the world. Like the gospel, the Flood both condemns and saves, depending on whether you are in the ark (Christ) or out of it.

As the Flood lifted Noah and his family up out of the world, even so does baptism now serve to save us out of the world. Properly seen, the act of baptism is a testimony of resignation from this world, a prophecy of the coming sentence of judgment upon our world, and an appeal to God for a good conscience via the resurrection of Jesus!

The water "saves" us in the sense that it is the line of separation. The baptized Christian has renounced the world; he can never have the same relationship with it that he once did.

We see this same idea in the story of the Exodus. The children of Israel never really left Egypt until they crossed the Red Sea. Through the water the separation became complete, for Egypt went in after them, but never came out of the sea, the waters having come down upon the "horses and riders" of Pharaoh.

- **The water prepared the way for a New Heavens and Earth.** There was a sense in which the world that Noah and his family stepped out of the ark into, was completely different from the world that they left to enter the ark. The canopy above their heads was replaced by sky and clouds. The weather would consequently be different. The topography of the earth would show the signs of cataclysm. The population of the earth would have been greatly reduced. Indeed, it was as though an eraser had wiped the slate clean (almost), and "all things" had now become "new".

Noah's ark and the new earth and heavens he stepped into, are dim types of what the ultimate plan of God is.

> And he that sat upon the throne said, **Behold, I make all things new**. And he said unto me, Write: for these words are true and faithful (Revelation 21:5).

God is going to "judge the world in righteousness", and ultimately destroy everything of this age of sin, death, corruption, and deceit. It is all dead and has to go. But first He is remaking the hearts of those He has redeemed, that we might be fit to take our place in His "New Heavens and the New Earth". *"If any man be in Christ, he is a new creation, the old has passed away, and all things have become new" (2 Corinthians 5:17).*

Everything that the water signifies in the story of Noah, the cross of Jesus, likewise signifies for us in our time. The cross is the revelation and instrument of divine wrath. It is our own flood, but poured out upon Jesus in our stead. It is also the saving and separating principle, as Paul the apostle said,

> But God forbid that I should glory, save in the cross of our Lord Jesus Christ, by whom the world is crucified unto me, and I unto the world. For in Christ Jesus neither circumcision availeth any thing, nor uncircumcision, but a new creature (Galatians 6:14-15).

And finally, the cross has made the way for God to inaugurate a new creation, wiping out the old—(We have died with Christ.)—and paying the price for sinners to be "born again" and partakers of the New Creation.

10

New Creation

And God remembered Noah, and every living thing, and all the cattle that was with him in the ark: and God made a wind to pass over the earth, and the waters assuaged; The fountains also of the deep and the windows of heaven were stopped, and the rain from heaven was restrained; And the waters returned from off the earth continually: and after the end of the hundred and fifty days the waters were abated. And the ark rested in the seventh month, on the seventeenth day of the month, upon the mountains of Ararat (Genesis 8:1-4).

OTHER THAN NOAH'S ARK, the face of the earth was just as it had been on the first day of Creation. Waters covered everything on earth. This is because God's holy judgment amounted to a reversal of His work in Creation. In Creation He separated the waters above and the waters below and the dry land. But the Flood reversed all of that.

In the judgment to come, we will see variations of the same phenomena; God will reverse His earlier works of Creation.

Revelation 16 is an amazing example of this. Whereas

once the LORD said, "Let there be light" . . . in the days to come, there shall be partial and then complete darkness covering the earth. The ocean, which He commanded to become filled with life, shall become a polluted sea of blood. The sun, nourisher and giver of life and light, will become man's enemy on that day. The day of the LORD's vengeance will be a day of "de-creation".

But after 150 days we are told that God "remembered Noah", and what remained of His living, breathing creation. The LORD did so in the sense that He began to act directly on their behalf. He marked that it was time for the flood waters to recede, and for Noah and his family to repopulate the earth.

The Lord closed the underground fountains, as well as the "windows of heaven" from further rain, and sent a drying wind *(ruach)* to blow over the face of the earth. This verse is reminiscent of Genesis 1. For in the Creation narrative we are told, "the Spirit *(Ruach)* of God brooded over the waters." The time had come for the (re)creation of a "new heavens and earth".

As to how the waters receded, other than the evaporative effects of the wind, we can only speculate. The massive underground storehouses of water which erupted at the time of the Flood, would have collapsed in places no doubt, no longer being filled with water, or perhaps they would have been refilled. Psalm 104 gives an intriguing hint at one possibility—a complete topographical change.

> Thou coveredst it (The earth) with the deep as with a garment: the waters stood above the mountains. At thy rebuke they fled; at the voice of thy thunder they hasted away. They go up by the mountains; they go down by the valleys unto the place which thou hast founded for them. Thou hast set a bound that they may not pass over; that they turn not again to cover the earth. He sendeth

the springs into the valleys, which run among the hills (Psalm 104:6-10).

The quote, *"They go up by the mountains; they go down by the valleys"* could better be rendered ***"The mountains go up and the valleys go down"***. The Flood affected an entirely new geography, moving water being the most powerful physical force on the earth, able to move and deposit massive amounts of sediment, and capable of eroding rock.

Everywhere we look on this earth we see the evidence of the cataclysm. The existence of fossils, the drainage erosion in places such as the Grand Canyon, the obviously congruent layers of sediment, some of it horizontally laid, but in other striking cases, obviously laid in layers and pushed up or down, wrinkled like blankets in a bed.

I quote Dr Henry Morris's commentary *The Genesis Record.*

> . . . a worldwide flood must have had worldwide geologic effects. Especially must this have been true in such a Flood as described in the Bible, caused by global eruptions, and downpours continuing for 150 days. Such a flood would have destroyed every earlier physiographic feature on or near the earth's surface, redepositing the eroded materials all over the earth in stratified sedimentary rocks of the earth's crust . . .

> Not only do such sedimentary rocks abound all over the world, but they give much evidence of having been formed by rapid and continous depositional processes. Each individual stratum is a distinct sedimentary unit and, in most formations, can be shown by hydraulic analysis to have been formed within a few minutes time . . .[19]

The apostle Peter tells us that the only way to *not* know

that there was at one time a cataclysm, would be to become "willfully ignorant" out of fear or rebellious refusal to face the implications of a previous worldwide divine judgment.

> This second epistle, beloved, I now write unto you; in both which I stir up your pure minds by way of remembrance: That ye may be mindful of the words which were spoken before by the holy prophets, and of the commandment of us the apostles of the Lord and Saviour: Knowing this first, that there shall come in the last days scoffers, walking after their own lusts, And saying, Where is the promise of his coming? for since the fathers fell asleep, all things continue as they were from the beginning of the creation. For this they willingly are ignorant of, that by the word of God the heavens were of old, and the earth standing out of the water and in the water: Whereby the world that then was, being overflowed with water, perished: But the heavens and the earth, which are now, by the same word are kept in store, reserved unto fire against the day of judgment and perdition of ungodly men. But, beloved, be not ignorant of this one thing, that one day is with the Lord as a thousand years, and a thousand years as one day. The Lord is not slack concerning his promise, as some men count slackness; but is longsuffering to us-ward, not willing that any should perish, but that all should come to repentance. But the day of the Lord will come as a thief in the night; in the which the heavens shall pass away with a great noise, and the elements shall melt with fervent heat, the earth also and the works that are therein shall be burned up (1 Peter 3:1-11).

<> <> <>

The Raven And The Dove

*And it came to pass at the end of forty days, that
Noah opened the window of the ark which he had
made: And he sent forth a raven, which went forth
to and fro, until the waters were dried up from off
the earth. Also he sent forth a dove from him, to see
if the waters were abated from off the face of the
ground; But the dove found no rest for the sole of
her foot, and she returned unto him into the ark,
for the waters were on the face of the whole earth:
then he put forth his hand, and took her, and pulled
her in unto him into the ark. And he stayed yet other
seven days; and again he sent forth the dove out of
the ark; And the dove came in to him in the evening;
and, lo, in her mouth was an olive leaf pluckt off:
so Noah knew that the waters were abated from
off the earth. And he stayed yet other seven days;
and sent forth the dove; which returned not again
unto him any more. And it came to pass in the six
hundredth and first year, in the first month, the first
day of the month, the waters were dried up from off
the earth: and Noah removed the covering of the
ark, and looked, and, behold, the face of the ground
was dry (Genesis 8:7-13).*

WE WERE ALREADY TOLD in Genesis 8:4 that the ark "rested"
on Mount Ararat. This is the second mention of rest in the
Bible. (The first, of God resting after six days of Creation).
The ark came to rest on the mountain after five months of
floating through the deluge and its aftermath. The ark is
a type of Christ. Jesus also saved the world, and then "sat

down at the right hand of the Father", entering into His rest.

But though the ark had now set down on Mount Ararat, Noah and the inhabitants of the ark could not yet disembark, for the flood was yet draining from the earth. It would take two and a half months before the mountain tops appeared above the floodwaters.

After another forty days, Noah opened the window at the top of the ark and released a raven. This raven was one of a set of two, an unclean bird, a scavenger. The raven flew from place to place, apparently able to perch on any rotten, bloated bodies of men or animals which yet floated on the surface of the waters.

One week later Noah released a dove, a clean bird, one from a set of seven pairs. (The reason there were seven pairs of "clean animals" to one pair of each unclean animal, was because of the need for sacrifice). The dove will not light upon anything dead or rotten. Therefore not yet finding any place to rest, the dove returned.

There is a pun here in the Hebrew text, for the word for rest, is *manoah,* thus literally, the dove *"found no manoah, so she returned"* to Noah.

One week later the dove was again released, but returned this time with a fresh olive leaf. This informed Noah that the waters had receded quite a bit, for olive trees don't grow at the higher altitudes of great mountains.

Seven days later the dove was released and didn't return to Noah, proving that the waters had sufficiently abated to allow the dove to nest. Thus the dove's mission was to verify that the judgment had ended, and that man could start all over again through Noah and his family.

Centuries later, at the River Jordan, John the Baptist witnessed the descent of the Holy Spirit, in the form of a Holy Dove, which lit upon Jesus as he was being baptized. The voice of the Father spoke from heaven, "***This is my beloved***

Son, in Him I am well **pleased".**

Eidersheim points out the typological significance of this beautifully, in his valuable *Life and Times of Jesus the Messiah.*

> **It was as if, symbolically, in the words of St. Peter, (1 Peter 3:21)** that Baptism had been a new flood, and He Who now emerged from it, the Noah – or rest, and comfort-bringer – Who took into His Ark the dove bearing the olive-branch, indicative of a new life. Here, at these waters, was the Kingdom, into which Jesus had entered in the **fulfilment of all righteousness; and from them he emerged as its Heaven-designated, Heaven-qualified, and Heaven-proclaimed King. As such he had received the fulness of the Spirit for His Messianic Work—a fulness abiding in Him—that out of it we might receive, and grace for grace.** [20]

Thus we see in Noah's ark, a foreshadowing of another ultimate, universal deliverance from God's wrath, and a new Ark, in the form of a Savior. This is the new Noah, the "rest bringer" upon whom the Holy Ghost of God can truly abide, and in whom all who seek refuge and cleansing from defilement, share in that same Spirit of sanctification and truth.

<> <> <>

And in the second month, on the seven and twentieth day of the month, was the earth dried. And God spake unto Noah, saying, Go forth of the ark, thou, and thy wife, and thy sons, and thy sons' wives with thee. Bring forth with thee every living thing that is with thee, of all flesh, both of fowl, and of cattle, and of every creeping thing that creepeth upon the earth; that they may breed abundantly in the earth,

and be fruitful, and multiply upon the earth. And Noah went forth, and his sons, and his wife, and his sons' wives with him: Every beast, every creeping thing, and every fowl, and whatsoever creepeth upon the earth, after their kinds, went forth out of the ark. And Noah builded an altar unto the Lord; and took of every clean beast, and of every clean fowl, and offered burnt offerings on the altar. And the Lord smelled a sweet savour; and the Lord said in his heart, I will not again curse the ground any more for man's sake; for the imagination of man's heart is evil from his youth; neither will I again smite any more every thing living, as I have done. While the earth remaineth, seedtime and harvest, and cold and heat, and summer and winter, and day and night shall not cease (Genesis 8: 14-22).

FINALLY, AFTER JUST A little more than a year since Noah and his family entered into the ark, the ordeal was over. The earth had dried sufficiently. It was time to come out of the ark. Notice the precision of language here—"the second month, the 27ᵗʰ of the month . . .". There is nothing figurative about this story. It happened in history, and in real-time and space. God once flooded the whole earth in judgment, but insured the continuity of the human race by preserving Noah and all life that breathes air.

Like a new corporate Adam, the little family, from which every one of earth's present 7.5 billions have descended, Noah and his wife and sons and their wives stepped off of the ark into a new world.

Like Adam also, they beheld a cavalcade of all of the land animals passing before them. This time not to name them, but to release them into the post-cataclysmic new geography, and to hear the divine charge together to *"be fruitful and multiply"* and fill the earth.

But the post-flood earth would be no Eden, for the judgment had brought about severe and lasting changes. No longer would the earth be shielded from direct sunlight by the vapor canopy over head, as the old world had. Consequently, men would not be able to live as long as formerly. God Himself had decreed that His Spirit would from then on, *"only strive with men"* for 120 years at the most.

Weather would be different also; the skies would be turbulent at times due to the swirling air currents, bringing varying levels of heat and cold into contact. Also there would be a buildup of snow and ice at the earth's poles; north and south would have extreme temperatures. The equator also would become a place of extreme heat. There would be seasons also, and that wouldn't change as long as the earth exists in the post-flood form.

The Flood created a whole new system of rugged mountain ranges, canyons and mesas, as an everlasting testimony to all men of the sheer power of God. Anyone can see the obvious water-created layers of sediment in places such as the at the Grand Canyon. The congruous pattern of the various layers of sediment are not all horizontal either. Some of them have been "wrinkled" and are in a grooved parallel pattern, having been formed as the earth's plates shifted while they were yet hardening almost as though blankets were laid out on top of each other, then wrinkled together.

The earth Noah stepped out into, was a different place from the earth he had lived in a year before. It was much more ominous, the signs of cataclysm all about him. There was a marked difference in lifespan, growing seasons and weather patterns that were unknown to him.

The only constant was his God.

So as the first human act in the renewed post-flood world, our father Noah and his family built an altar and made sacrifice of the clean animals God had provided. He offered propitiation, that is a satisfaction offering, a substitute for the sins of the remaining human race, i.e., Noah, his wife, his sons and their wives. No doubt he also offered peace offerings; thus by sacrifice, at this point the entire human race entered into fellowship with God, on God's holy terms of sacrifice, atonement, and propitiation.

Finally, I'm sure he offered a thanksgiving sacrifice, out of sheer gratitude that he and his family were not swept into perdition with the wicked.

God smelled the sweet-smelling savor. That is, He received the prayers and worship of Noah because of the substitute. Noah's primal sacrifice pointed ahead to the ultimate propitiation, and the basis for salvation, the self-offering of Jesus Christ.

> Be ye therefore followers of God, as dear children; And walk in love, as Christ also hath loved us, and hath given himself for us an offering and a sacrifice to God for a sweetsmelling savour (Ephesians 5:1-2.)

Noah no doubt prayed not only for himself, his wife, sons and their wives, but for his descendants also. God heard Noah's prayer and decreed that He would never again destroy all life on the entire earth as He had done. When God promised never to curse the earth again, it didn't mean that the curse of Genesis 3:21 was now revoked, but that the additional curse which brought the Flood would never be revisited.

The reason God gave for vowing never to destroy all life, is the fact that God knows that men's thoughts are only evil continually. In other words, because men have original sin, and their thoughts always tend towards evil, God would deal with us in mercy.

All of His dealings have an element of mercy. The shortening of men's lives is mercy. The continuity of seasons is mercy. So also would be His next decrees, a re-ordering of the human/animal relationship, and the establishment of human government to preserve some semblance of order.

God is good, and His mercy is everlasting!

11

The New Order

And God blessed Noah and his sons, and said unto them, Be fruitful, and multiply, and replenish the earth. And the fear of you and the dread of you shall be upon every beast of the earth, and upon every fowl of the air, upon all that moveth upon the earth, and upon all the fishes of the sea; into your hand are they delivered. Every moving thing that liveth shall be meat for you; even as the green herb have I given you all things. But flesh with the life thereof, which is the blood thereof, shall ye not eat. And surely your blood of your lives will I require; at the hand of every beast will I require it, and at the hand of man; at the hand of every man's brother will I require the life of man. Whoso sheddeth man's blood, by man shall his blood be shed: for in the image of God made he man. And you, be ye fruitful, and multiply; bring forth abundantly in the earth, and multiply therein (Genesis 9:1-6).

THIS *INCLUSIO*, (PASSAGE WHICH BEGINS AND ends virtually the same way), outlines the new order established by God upon the earth, affecting the relations between humans and animals, as well as establishing human government on the earth.

Of first importance, as indicted by repetition at the end of the passage, is that man is still called to *be fruitful, and multiply and to replenish and cultivate the earth.* Though his imagination is evil continually (original sin), there is yet a future for man. He is to bear children, grow, and derive abundance from the earth. He is to expand in number and settle, occupy, and cultivate the earth to the glory of God.

Contrast this with the modern Zero Population Growth ideal of our modern "thinkers", and with the devastation wrought by fifty years of a "birth control" and abortion revolution. Genesis 9 offers man the vision of life and hope, but the vision of our modern neo Eugenicists, is the vision of death and despair! How true Proverbs 8 is when it portrays personified Wisdom as saying, "*All those who hate me, love death!*"

Secondly, there is to be a clear difference between animal and human life. God would put the fear of man in all of the wild beasts, as a protection for man. Morris notes in his Genesis commentary that the domesticated animals are exempted from this stark terror. Man is still to rule over God's creation, but not by direct authority, as Adam once did, but indirectly through this fear.

Thirdly, for the first time in history, man was now authorized to use animals as a food source; man could now eat meat. There could be practical reasons for this, for now the harsh weather would perhaps require of man more protein for nourishment, especially dealing with winter cold. Or this allowance could have been given to reinforce the superiority of man over animals, a kind of brutal dominion!

There is a redemptive lesson to be gained in the eating of meat. The whole idea of substitutionary atonement is implicitly taught in it. For example, when the children of Israel were taught by God to keep the Passover, they were instructed to take a lamb into their house for three days (long enough to attach to it as a pet), then to slay it, roast it, and eat it as a family.

> Speak ye unto all the congregation of Israel, saying, In the tenth day of this month they shall take to them every man a lamb, according to the house of their fathers, a lamb for an house: ... Your lamb shall be without blemish, a male of the first year: ye shall take it out from the sheep, or from the goats: And ye shall keep it up until the fourteenth day of the same month: and the whole assembly of the congregation of Israel shall kill it in the evening. And they shall take of the blood, and strike it on the two side posts and on the upper door post of the houses, wherein they shall eat it (Genesis 12:3-7).

Those children were being taught that "that lamb had to die in order for us to live". A life given in exchange for a life, and sustenance and nourishment comes through that life substitute.

There is a spirituality to eating meat, which is perhaps why we are warned of the new false religion of the last days, which includes a "religious vegetarianism" among its other poisonous doctrines.

> Now the Spirit speaketh expressly, that in the latter times some shall depart from the faith, giving heed to seducing spirits, and doctrines of devils; Speaking lies in hypocrisy; having their conscience seared with a hot iron; Forbidding to marry, and **commanding to abstain from meats**, which God hath created to be received with thanksgiving of them which believe and know the truth. For every creature of God is good, and nothing to be refused, if it be received with thanksgiving (1Timothy 4:1-4).

Finally, though animal flesh could now be consumed, all blood itself was to be held sacred. The very *life of the flesh is in the blood.* All life belongs to God, the giver of life. The blood of clean animals would be used for sacrifice at God's command and was acceptable to God, until the coming of the antitype to all sacrifice, Jesus Christ.

Therefore out of reverence for the very principle of life and atoning sacrifice, the eating or drinking of blood was forbidden to man. This prohibition carries over into the New Testament as well, as the church council in Acts 15 attested, binding Gentile converts from blood consumption, whilst loosing them from circumcision.

> Wherefore my sentence is, that we trouble not them, which from among the Gentiles are turned to God: But that we write unto them, that they abstain from pollutions of idols, and from fornication, and from things strangled, and from blood (Acts 15:19-20).

As we will see in the next section, if animal blood was regarded by our Creator as sacred, how much more does He regard the sanctity of human blood?

> *And God blessed Noah and his sons, and said unto them, Be fruitful, and multiply, and replenish the earth . . . And surely your blood of your lives will I require; at the hand of every beast will I require it, and at the hand of man; at the hand of every man's brother will I require the life of man. Whoso sheddeth man's blood, by man shall his blood be shed: for in the image of God made he man. And you, be ye fruitful, and multiply; bring forth abundantly in the earth, and multiply therein (Genesis 9:1-7).*

Noah stepped out of the ark with his family into an entirely new world. The cataclysm had radically transformed earth's geography in ways that are still manifestly obvious to anyone. Even the atmosphere was altered; new weather, seasonal changes, fluctuating temperatures, violent storms and direct exposure to sunlight, created an entirely new environment for the eight survivors of the Flood.

The Lord also ordained new ordinances governing the natural order, and man's relationship to animal life. Now there would be distinct seasons till the end of the world. Fear of man, would be instilled into the hearts of the wild animals, as a protection to man. Men were now permitted to use animals for food also, but the sanctity of life as a principle would be upheld, for eating or drinking blood was forbidden.

An altar was the first structure erected on the new earth, and a special kind of animal sacrifice was the first act of the first family of the new world. The word used for the offering is different from the one used previously. Abel offered a *minchah,* that is a "gift" to God from the altar. But the word for the sacrifice Noah offered is *olah,* that is, *"ascending".* The whole burnt offering of clean animals as a substitute, ascended unto God, with the prayers and worship of the pious, for God is above, and prayer is ever the upward look and the baring of the soul to Him who dwells on high.

The text notes that the Lord responded to this "sweet smelling savor" and from thence decreed the whole new order, natural and human, that the world might be preserved. All of the ordained sacrifices ultimately point to the one sufficient and saving sacrifice, that of the God-appointed Lamb, slain from the beginning, for the sins of all men.

Out of the primacy of worship and salvation by substitution, did the original civil order for mankind arise--the only legitimate order which consists of the priorities of God first, man second.

The divine decree commanding capital punishment of murderers, (*"He who sheds man's blood, by man shall his blood be shed"*), contained the seed germ of all true human civil order. It implied the idea of delegated governmental authority. It also implied human courts, judges, agreed upon legal sanctions, investigation into crimes, and eventually became embodied in the legitimate State.

> Let every soul be subject unto the higher powers. For there is no power but of God: the powers that be are ordained of God. Whosoever therefore resisteth the power, resisteth the ordinance of God: and they that resist shall receive to themselves damnation. For rulers are not a terror to good works, but to the evil. Wilt thou then not be afraid of the power? do that which is good, and thou shalt have praise of the same: For he is the minister of God to thee for good. But if thou do that which is evil, be afraid; for he beareth not the sword in vain: for he is the minister of God, a revenger to execute wrath upon him that doeth evil (Romans 13:1-4).

Government has a legitimate God-assigned function, which is the restraint of evil. Up to this time, there had not been a human government. Man was given the chance to see what would happen should there be no human restraints, nor time restraints on human nature, in the centuries leading to the Flood. From this time forth, in mercy God appointed human government, and has given it a sword to restrain evil.

The basis for the imposition of the death penalty for murderers is contained in a simple decree of God, with implications that could fill encyclopedias. *"Whoso sheddeth man's blood, by man shall his blood be shed: for in the image of God made he man."*

As Sauer put it in *The Dawn of World Redemption,*

> But since the death penalty upon the murderer is
> based upon the likeness to God of the murdered
> (Genesis 9:6) this indicates that the exercise of
> justice must be practiced upon the principle of
> acknowledgement of man in the Image of God,
> and by consequence of the mental and spiritual
> nobility of man. Therefore must the authority
> must depend not upon brute force, but on the
> acknowledgment of the Divinely granted natural
> right in human society . . .[21]

What happens to society when the idea of man made in
the image of God is repudiated, forgotten, or lost? We are
beginning to see, and the picture isn't pretty—oppression,
injustice, abortion, two tiered justice, arbitrary and chang-
ing standards of justice.

What happens when a society believes itself too compassionate for the death penalty? When they think they can
improve upon God in the area of compassion? We are living
the nightmare, as life is cheapened, murderers are let off
after a few years, and the streets of our cities become nightmare war zones such as Detroit or Chicago.

Ironically, often the same people who think capital punishment for murderers, kidnappers and rapists, is too barbaric, have no problem with the practice of abortion. Thus
they impose a death penalty upon the most innocent, and
mercy on the blood guilty. True is the Proverb which declares, *"the tender mercies of the wicked are cruel."*

<> <> <>

And God spake unto Noah, and to his sons with
him, saying, And I, behold, I establish my covenant
with you, and with your seed after you; And with
every living creature . . . And I will establish my

covenant with you, neither shall all flesh be cut off any more by the waters of a flood; neither shall there any more be a flood to destroy the earth. And God said, This is the token of the covenant which I make between me and you and every living creature that is with you, for perpetual generations: I do set my bow in the cloud, and it shall be for a token of a covenant between me and the earth. And it shall come to pass, when I bring a cloud over the earth, that the bow shall be seen in the cloud: And I will remember my covenant, which is between me and you and every living creature . . . And the bow shall be in the cloud; and I will look upon it, that I may remember the everlasting covenant between God and every living creature of all flesh that is upon the earth (Genesis 9:8-16).

As we have stated, as they stepped off of the ark into the cataclysmically transformed earth, Noah and his family would have seen radical environmental changes. There was no longer a canopy of vapor above them, now they would be exposed to direct sunlight. Instead clouds roiled over head.

As the storm clouds receded and the sun gleamed through the clouds, a stunning sevenfold prism of color appeared in the form of an arc over the earth. The new conditions allowed for the appearance of the rainbow.

God told Noah that the rainbow was the token and sign of His unconditional covenant with the earth itself and with every living creature, that never again would He flood the whole earth, cutting off all life on earth. As long as the earth remains in its present form, never again would He smite every living thing; life would continue till the final consummation of all things.

Not only would man see the token, but God says that He would see it, and remind Himself of this covenant of mercy. In fact both Ezekiel and John the Apostle tell us that they saw in their visions of God, that a rainbow completely surrounds God's throne in heaven.

> As the appearance of the bow that is in the cloud in the day of rain, so was the appearance of the brightness round about. This was the appearance of the likeness of the glory of the Lord. And when I saw it, I fell upon my face, and I heard a voice of one that spake (Ezekiel 1:28).

> And immediately I was in the spirit: and, behold, a throne was set in heaven, and one sat on the throne. And he that sat was to look upon like a jasper and a sardine stone: and there was a rainbow round about the throne, in sight like unto an emerald (Revelation 4:2-3).

In every direction that God looks, He sees us through the prism of mercy. The rainbow looks like a bridge from heaven to earth. God calls it "My bow", and promises to look at it and remember to have mercy on sinful man. In a beautiful way, the rainbow is a teaching about the grace of God. After the terrible storm, glory! In judgment and wrath, He remembers mercy.

The rainbow is a divine sermon that God is not willing that any should perish but that all should come to repentance. Like the stars, it is a testimony to the glory and beauty of God. The pure, white light which streams from His Holy presence is filtered and separated through the glorious cloud which stands between God and man, yet flowing through to this sinful world in stunningly beautiful prime colors.

Here on earth, we only see half of the bow, for we know

only in part here, and see through a glass darkly; but the bow is a complete circle in heaven, around the throne of the Father. Love, beauty and holy generosity truly triumph over human sinfulness and guilt.

The rainbow testifies powerfully for all who have eyes to see and ears to hear, that there truly is a higher, purer and better city for all of us!

<> <> <>

And Noah began to be an husbandman, and he planted a vineyard: And he drank of the wine, and was drunken; and he was uncovered within his tent. And Ham, the father of Canaan, saw the nakedness of his father, and told his two brethren without. And Shem and Japheth took a garment, and laid it upon both their shoulders, and went backward, and covered the nakedness of their father; and their faces were backward, and they saw not their father's nakedness. And Noah awoke from his wine, and knew what his younger son had done unto him. And he said, Cursed be Canaan; a servant of servants shall he be unto his brethren. And he said, Blessed be the Lord God of Shem; and Canaan shall be his servant. God shall enlarge Japheth, and he shall dwell in the tents of Shem; and Canaan shall be his servant. And Noah lived after the flood three hundred and fifty years (Genesis 9:20-28).

LIKE A NEW ADAM, Noah stepped off of the ark into a new "heavens and earth". All of us who live in the post-Flood world descend from Noah, so in that way also he is a type of Adam. As all of humanity was "in Adam" in the garden, so all post-Flood humanity were in the ark in Noah or his three sons.

We come now to the account of the "fall" of the new Adam, this time brought about not by forbidden fruit, but by drink.

Noah drank wine, and in his excess he passed out naked within his own tent. This unfortunate incident proved to be a test of the character of Noah's three sons. What do you do when you discover "the nakedness" of someone set over you?

Ham drew attention to it, calling his brothers into the tent to behold their father in this state of humiliation. Shem and Japheth wanted to preserve their father's dignity, refusing to behold their father in such a state.

We have to look at the biblical view of what nakedness means in order to truly understand this story. In divine revelation, clothing has a practical function, but also it has to do with the concept of dignity, honor and authority. Thus, the exposure of someone's nakedness has to with the diminishment and even the possible removal of respect and honor.

Ham didn't necessarily do anything sexual to his father, but the desire he demonstrated for his brothers to see the spectacle of the nakedness of their own father, reveals a resentful desire to see his father's honor diminished. It was an attempt to "take the old man down a few notches" in the esteem of his brothers. In other words, it was an expression of rebellion, and resentment of his father's authority.

When Shem and Japheth did the opposite of Ham, not only were they honoring Noah their father by refusing to entertain a degraded image of him, they were honoring the God of their father as well.

Likewise Ham's act of rebellion, seeking to show his father in a diminished light, revealed a heart that was already defecting from the God of Noah. The phrase *"Ham ... told his brothers"*, literally means *"told his brothers with delight"*. He assumed that they also would find some kind of pleasure in the degraded expose of their father also.

When Noah woke out of his drunken stupor, he soon realized, *"what his younger son had done to him"*.

The ensuing prophecy, was directed first to Ham, (although spoken to Ham's son Canaan), then Shem and Japheth.

Why was the curse directed to Canaan? He didn't say, *"Cursed be Canaan"*, but *"Cursed **is** Canaan"*. It was not a deterministic prophecy, but a prophetic observation. Noah could see by the spirit of prophecy that the perverse streak of rebellion revealed in Ham, was already rapidly progressing in Canaan, and would ultimately consume his descendants.

Such rebellion would only lead to servitude. *"A servant of servants shall he be . . ."* It is important to note that this is not the so-called curse on the Negro race. There is no such thing. Ham had four sons, Phut, Mizraim, Cush, and Canaan. And Canaan, who was the youngest son, was the only one in Ham's family who was cursed.

To Shem, Noah prophesied, *"Blessed be the Lord God of Shem."* The Semitic people would be the custodians of the knowledge and name of God, for he literally uses the covenant name—*"Blessed be Jahweh, the Elohim of Shem"*. Shem knew the Lord by covenant.

It is interesting that the three major, monotheistic religions which have strongly influenced the world, come from the Semitic people: Judaism and Christianity of course, and the distortion of those two, Mohammedism.

But Noah repeated the earlier curse, *"And Canaan shall be His servant"*, which at the time of the writing of Genesis, was in process of fulfillment. The Canaanites had subdued the land given to Abraham, Isaac, and Jacob, building cities and clearing fields which Israel was soon to inhabit.

To Japheth the Word of the Lord comes as a pun, for Japheth means expander. *"God shall expand the expander . . ."* The Japhetic nations would explore, colonize, and spread out across the earth, both geographically and intellectually. The entire Western Hemisphere was discovered, colonized and developed by the sons of Japheth.

But Japheth would *"dwell in the tents of Shem".* That is, his people would be largely impacted by the revelation given to Shem, and thus share in the spirituality of Shem, worshipping his God, appropriating his blessings, and as it turns out, allowing the book of revelation of Shem's God, the Bible to affect his civilization. To this day we speak of our Judeo-Christian Western culture.

The order of these sons of Noah, in the prophecy is telling. Ham wasn't mentioned at all; his son Canaan is. Then Shem and finally Japheth. The divine record tells us that the earliest world empires were Hamitic, including Egypt. Then for a brief time Shem's descendants built world dominating civilizations such as the Sumerians and Babylonians.

But at the end, the world is dominated largely by Japheth's children—from Persia, to Greece to Rome and the West.

The Book of Acts has three individual conversion stories, showing the universality of the gospel. In Acts 8 a son of Ham comes to saving faith in Jesus, the Ethiopian eunuch. In Acts 9 we hear the story of Saul of Tarsus a Jew (Semite). Finally, we read of the conversion of Cornelius in Acts 10, a Roman son of Japheth. Jesus died for all of us sons of Adam!

There is much about this mysterious chapter I do not yet grasp, and admittedly this telling leaves as many questions as it does answers. But we can't force Scripture; we can only wait to receive fuller revelation.

12
The Table Of Nations

Now these are the generations of the sons of Noah, Shem, Ham, and Japheth: and unto them were sons born after the flood. The sons of Japheth; Gomer, and Magog, and Madai, and Javan, and Tubal, and Meshech, and Tiras. And the sons of Gomer; Ashkenaz, and Riphath, and Togarmah. And the sons of Javan; Elishah, and Tarshish, Kittim, and Dodanim. By these were the isles of the Gentiles divided in their lands; every one after his tongue, after their families, in their nations (Genesis 10:1-5).

WE COME TO THE "Table of Nations", which has been described even by unbelieving "higher critics" of Scripture, as a remarkably accurate, and unique historical document. This divine family record is the connecting genealogical path from the immediate aftermath of the Flood, to the emergence of the various nations which we see in biblical history.[22]

Humanity as we know it has a threefold root system, for we all trace back either to Shem, Ham or Japheth. There are no "races", for behind those three, we all descend from Noah, and from Adam before him.

The Table starts with Japheth, and his seven sons.

Gomer—The descendants of this son of Japheth eventually settled north of the Black Sea in a district which was called *Cimmeria,* and even today is known as *Crimea.* It is possible that the name of *Gomer* also survives in the name of the *Germanic* peoples.

Gomer's three sons were, *Ashkenaz, Riphath,* and *Togarmah. Ashkenaz* is definitely associated with the Germans. The Jews call German Jews, *Ashekenazi.* It is also possible that the name *Riphath* is preserved in the name of *Europe,* the continent which was predominantly settled by the sons of *Japheth.* The Armenian and Turkik peoples around the *Caspian Sea* and the *Caucus* mountains descend from *Togarmeh.*

Magog—This name can mean "The place of Gog". Magog was believed to be the ancestor of the Scythians, the original settlers around the Black Sea area.

Madai—Madai is the father of the Medes, who dwelt in what is now known as Persia and eventually intermarried with the Elamites (Semitic) to become the ancestors of the Persian people. The sons of Madai also inhabited the Indian subcontinent, the Indo-Aryan peoples descending from them. The Aryans of India have always insisted that their ancestor was a man named "Iyepti", which is perhaps a corruption of Japheth.

Javan—The son of Japheth, whose name was eventually pronounced Ionias went on to become the Greek nation, settling by the Aegian Sea and in Asia Minor (Turkey). Javan's children are also listed: Elisha, Tarshish, Kittim, and Dodanim. The name Elisha would become Hellas, from which the term Hellenistic, or the geographical name Hellespont derives.

The Roman people in their time of idolatry worshipped "Jupiter" as chief god, a possible corruption of the name of their ancestor, Japheth.

Tarshish would settle in North Africa, (Carthage) and in Spain, (Tartessos), but eventually Phoenicia. Kittim would be associated with those who settled the Cypriot Islands and the Greek mainland also. Dodanim may have given his name to the straits of the Dardenelles.

Tubal and Meshech—Both of these are usually associated together in the Bible. They originated in and around the area we now call Turkey, and spread out as far as the Caucasus Mountains, and the Georgian and Armenian areas.

Tiras—Josephus tells us that Tiras gave descent to the Thracian peoples. Possibly the Etruscans of Italy came from him as well.

Noah predicted that Japheth, "the expander" would expand, and thus he did both geographically, colonially, culturally, philosophically, and intellectually. It is of interest that to this day, it is Western civilization which is dominant in the world for good and evil.

It is also of interest that in the predictions of the final battles, the very names of the sons and grandchildren of Japheth re-emerge as participants in the final Gentile attempt to wipe out Israel and overthrow Israel's God.

> Son of man, set thy face against Gog, the land of Magog, the chief prince of Meshech and Tubal, and prophesy against him, And say, Thus saith the Lord God; Behold, I am against thee, O Gog, the chief prince of Meshech and Tubal: And I will turn thee back, and put hooks into thy jaws, and I will bring thee forth, and all thine army, horses and horsemen, all of them clothed with all sorts of armour, even a great company with bucklers and shields, all of them handling swords: Persia, Ethiopia, and Libya with them; all of them with shield and helmet: Gomer, and all his bands; the house of Togarmah of the north quarters, and all his bands: and many people with thee (Ezekiel 38:2-6).

<> <> <>

And the sons of Ham; Cush, and Mizraim, and
Phut, and Canaan. And the sons of Cush; Seba, and
Havilah, and Sabtah, and Raamah, and Sabtechah:
and the sons of Raamah; Sheba, and Dedan. And
Cush begat Nimrod: he began to be a mighty one in
the earth. He was a mighty hunter before the Lord:
wherefore it is said, Even as Nimrod the mighty
hunter before the Lord. And the beginning of his
kingdom was Babel, and Erech, and Accad, and
Calneh, in the land of Shinar (Genesis 10:6-10).

NOAH'S SON HAM HAD four sons: Cush, Mizraim, Phut, and
Canaan.

Special attention is focused on the line of Cush. His
sons were Seba, Havilah, Sabtah, Raamah, and Sabtecha.
Raamah's two sons were Seba and Dedan. Cush settled in
southern Arabia and in Ethiopia. Seba and Dedan also locat-
ed on the Arabian Peninsula.

But the text draws our attention to one other son of
Cush—Nimrod, whose name means "let us rebel". Nimrod
settled in the land of Shinar, that is between the Tigris and
the Euphrates rivers, and founded the world's first great
empire, known by modern archeologists as Sumeria.

Nimrod was said to begin "*to be a mighty one in the*
earth". In other words, Nimrod would be the first of a long
line of powerful despots. Nimrod is furthermore described
as being a "*mighty hunter before the Lord*". In fact it became
a proverb, "*As Nimrod, a mighty hunter before the Lord*". But
what does it mean, this two-part saying, that actually entered into the minds and mouths of the common man, as
an adage, "*Nimrod, a mighty hunter*" and "*before the Lord*"?

That Nimrod was a mighty hunter, does not refer to the pastime of hunting wild game, rather he was as a king, a conqueror. He took cities, territories and peoples. *"Before the Lord"* at first glance is obvious. God sees everything everyone does, and takes note for the Day of Judgment. But there is more to the saying than that, for it also indicates a radical separation from the Lord. In the modern vernacular it could be paraphrased, *"in the very face of the Lord"*, or even, *"in defiance of the Lord"*.

Thus the power and prowess of Nimrod and his open defiance of the God of Shem, made him wildly popular with many of his contemporaries, so much so that his rebellion became a byword in the ancient world.

> *Out of that land went forth Asshur, and builded Nineveh, and the city Rehoboth, and Calah, And Resen between Nineveh and Calah: the same is a great city. And Mizraim begat Ludim, and Anamim, and Lehabim, and Naphtuhim, And Pathrusim, and Casluhim, (out of whom came Philistim,) and Caphtorim.*

Ham's other sons founded great civilizations, settling in all of Africa, Arabia and the land of Canaan and, as seafaring Phoenicians and Philistines, built cities around the Mediterranean.

> *And Canaan begat Sidon his first-born, and Heth, And the Jebusite, and the Amorite, and the Girgasite, And the Hivite, and the Arkite, and the Sinite, And the Arvadite, and the Zemarite, and the Hamathite: and afterward were the families of the Canaanites spread abroad. And the border of the Canaanites was from Sidon, as thou comest*

> to Gerar, unto Gaza; as thou goest, unto Sodom,
> and Gomorrah, and Admah, and Zeboim, even
> unto Lasha. These are the sons of Ham, after their
> families, after their tongues, in their countries, and
> in their nations (Genesis 10:15-20).

Mizraim founded Egypt. Phut settled west of Egypt in what is now known as Libya. Mizraim's son Pathrusim founded Pathros. The Philistines descend from Ham, through Mizraim's son Casluhim.

Finally Canaan settled in what is now known as the Holy Land. Canaan had a son Sidon whose name survived in the city-state on the coast of Lebanon.

Genesis 10 tells us that "and afterwards were the families of Canaan spread abroad". Henry Morris speculates that,

> This suggests the intriguing possibility that cer-
> tain groups of Canaanites (notably the Hittites
> and perhaps also the Sinites, whose very name
> suggests China) may have spread over into the
> great Asian Continent as well. The record does say
> that of the three sons of Noah, "The whole earth
> was overspread" (Genesis 9:19).[23]

We do know that everyone on earth is traceable to at least one of these three sons of Noah, and that the nations were formed and divided that men may seek God.

> And hath made of one blood all nations of men
> for to dwell on all the face of the earth, and hath
> determined the times before appointed, and the
> bounds of their habitation; That they should seek
> the Lord, if haply they might feel after him, and
> find him, though he be not far from every one of
> us (Acts 17:25-26).

<> <> <>

Unto Shem also, the father of all the children of Eber, the brother of Japheth the elder, even to him were children born. The children of Shem; Elam, and Asshur, and Arphaxad, and Lud, and Aram. And the children of Aram; Uz, and Hul, and Gether, and Mash. And Arphaxad begat Salah; and Salah begat Eber. And unto Eber were born two sons: the name of one was Peleg; for in his days was the earth divided; and his brother's name was Joktan. And Joktan begat Almodad, and Sheleph, and Hazarmaveth, and Jerah, And Hadoram, and Uzal, and Diklah, And Obal, and Abimael, and Sheba, And Ophir, and Havilah, and Jobab: all these were the sons of Joktan. And their dwelling was from Mesha, as thou goest unto Sephar a mount of the east. These are the sons of Shem, after their families, after their tongues, in their lands, after their nations. These are the families of the sons of Noah, after their generations, in their nations: and by these were the nations divided in the earth after the flood.(Genesis 10:21-32)

Concerning the sons of Shem, the rest of Genesis focuses on this line, through which the "seed of the woman" was destined to come. Of particular interest is the family of Eber. Both Shem and Eber would have been alive when Abraham was born. Eber, the ancestor of Abraham, is possibly where the name "Hebrew" comes from.

Shem's two Elam and Asshur are the forefathers of the Elamites (Persians) and the Assyrians. His son Aram became the Arameans (Syrians). Shem's son Arphaxad is in the line of the Messiah, the seed of the woman as are Arphaxad's grandson Selah and his great grandson Eber, who was mentioned at first. Eber bore two sons, Peleg and Joktan.

Peleg, which means "divided" was so named because in his time the peoples of the earth were divided by language. Further down the line of Shem, comes Terah, who had a son, Abraham. Scripture focuses in on that line of Abraham, Isaac and Jacob for obvious reasons for the rest of Genesis.

13

The Apostasy

And the whole earth was of one language, and of one speech. And it came to pass, as they journeyed from the east, that they found a plain in the land of Shinar; and they dwelt there. And they said one to another, Go to, let us make brick, and burn them thoroughly. And they had brick for stone, and slime had they for morter. And they said, Go to, let us build us a city and a tower, whose top may reach unto heaven; and let us make us a name, lest we be scattered abroad upon the face of the whole earth (Genesis 11:1-4).

GENESIS 11 TAKES A closer look at events alluded to in the previous chapter, i.e., the references to the rise of the tyrant Nimrod, (whose name means, "let us rebel"), and to Peleg, of whom it was said that in his time the earth was divided. The cause and nature of that division is the subject of chapter 11.

At this time the tribes of Shem, Ham and Japheth had not yet spread out over the earth, as God had commanded them to do. Rather it seems that they banded together in the city named "Babel", which is interpreted as "gate of the gods", in the land of Shinar in southern Mesopotamia. The word "Shinar" means "casting down".

The apostasy, which involved virtually the entire population of the world, centered around three things.

- **A city**—The city was already built, of course, Babel, Nimrod's capital. It became the focal point for the universal rebellion against the God who told them to go out and to subdue and fill the earth. They would not spread out, nor would they pioneer to subdue the earth. Rather, they would collectivize, joining hand in hand to live on their own terms without God.

Like their ancestor Cain, who founded a city after slaying his brother, naming it Enoch, ("inauguration"), the city Babel became the "new beginning" of life for the united world away from the God of Shem.

- **A tower**—Central to the new world-uniting city, was a tower, "Whose top would reach unto heaven". There are several plausible theories about the meaning of the tower. Some say it was a safeguard against the possibility of another flood. As if the priests of Babel were saying, *"This time some of us, (the elite) will survive, by seeking refuge on top of the tower. We can't ever allow the God of the flood to wipe us out again!".*

Another theory—one that I find most plausible—is that the tower was a pyramid or ziggurat, which elevated a platform for priests to better observe the planets in order that they might practice astrology.

There is a third theory, that the tower represented heaven. The ancients would create their own symbolic cosmological "heaven" on high platforms, so that through ritual performance, man would be in control of what happens in heaven and subsequently, on earth.

The truth could be any one of these or any combination of them. The effect was that man would be in control of his own life, and be the one to define and create his own destiny. Shem's God wouldn't be needed anymore, nor would He have to be feared, now that they had the unity and technology to make their own way.

- **A name**—Underlying the tower and city building project, was the deepest reason for the apostasy, for they would "*make a name*" for themselves. This is another way of saying that they wanted to be independent of God. They wanted to redefine themselves in terms of their humanity and to divorce themselves from the God of heaven, Shem and the Flood.

The fact that God named Adam, and calls men by their names, implies His dominion over them. The object named belongs to the one who named it. There is accountability also, for the namer defines the named. When God allowed Adam to name the animals, He was giving man dominion over them.

The city and tower building project was a revolt against God, a rejection of accountability to, and definition by the Creator of the universe. At that time man was absolutely united in rebellion and repudiation of God. All spoke the same language and virtually all had adopted the rebellious mindset.

In order to accomplish their goals, the leaders set out to utilize technology and to organize labor, to mass-produce bricks, and to harvest bitumen for mortar for the project. Nothing would be spared in this monumental undertaking, all men worked together in a remarkable spirit of unity.

The making of bricks, i.e., artificial stones, all uniform, to the same standards, sizes and weights has a symbolic meaning in Scripture. A stone represents truth, thus the

Ten Commandments are etched into stone tablets. Bricks are manmade, and represent falsity. The temple was made of stone, not brick. Pharaoh forced the children of Israel to make bricks.

Bricks represent man's technology to make his own world. The conformity of bricks as opposed to stone seems to be a good metaphor for the manmade unity, the one size fits all, no distinctions, multi-cultural world we are constructing, in which no one is "right" or "wrong". Nothing is distinct. All is one.

Isn't this what we in the modern world desperately want? Isn't the idea of all men communicating and working together in one common cause, one of our highest ideals? How many popular modern songs have pined for an ideal world in which we all "love one another", and work for the common good, and in which there are no separate nations, no wars, no barriers, nothing to keep men apart?

Haven't we always wanted to *"teach the world to sing in perfect harmony"*? To Imagine a world *"as one"*, in which there is *"nothing to live for, or to die for"*? How different are God's ideals from man's! Our Savior has told us, *". . . that which is highly esteemed among men is abomination in the sight of God."*

At the height of the idyllic world unity project, God Himself *"came down"* out of concern for man, to see for Himself this project and to determine the best course of action to utterly destroy it.

<> <> <>

And the whole earth was of one language, and of one speech. And it came to pass, as they journeyed from the east, that they found a plain in the land of Shinar; and they dwelt there. And they said one to another, Go to, let us make brick, and burn them

*thoroughly. And they had brick for stone, and slime
had they for morter. And they said, Go to, let us
build us a city and a tower, whose top may reach
unto heaven; and let us make us a name, lest we
be scattered abroad upon the face of the whole
earth. And the Lord came down to see the city and
the tower, which the children of men builded. And
the Lord said, Behold, the people is one, and they
have all one language; and this they begin to do:
and now nothing will be restrained from them,
which they have imagined to do. Go to, let us go
down, and there confound their language, that
they may not understand one another's speech. So
the Lord scattered them abroad from thence
upon the face of all the earth: and they left off to
build the city. Therefore is the name of it called
Babel; because the Lord did there confound the
language of all the earth: and from thence did
the Lord scatter them abroad upon the face of all
the earth (Genesis 11:1-9).*

IT SOUNDED GOOD IN theory; all men on earth working together on the same project, towards the same end--a tower
and a city to represent a complete world unity. There were
no separate nations, or cultures, no language barriers, no
competing factions. There was no such thing as "diversity".
In fact the unity was amazing, the like of which has not been
seen since!

All men worked together to make the world a better
place, or perhaps to make it a safer place for man. Humanity was functioning as a productive, collective, highly organized unit, set to one great task under capable leadership!
The whole world was "one"!

But God didn't see it that way.

The Lord came down to see the city and the tower... That is, the LORD condescended to evaluate this work of man, for judgment. He who already knows all things, nonetheless "came down" to see this spectacle from the perspective of a man—shadows of the incarnation and vicarious substitution of our Lord.

It wasn't good at all that all men spoke the same language, and were engaged in a universal world improvement project, with no differences, cultural or otherwise to present any barriers to them. Man is fallen, therefore the complete pooling of man's intellect and his strength and willingness to undertake a global project under a one world governance can only lead men further away from God.

Now nothing will be restrained from them, which they have imagined to do...

Without the above mentioned barriers, there is no stopping man in his elaborate defection from God. When "hand joins in hand" among the fallen ones, unity is their undoing, for they drag each other down to hell. If man could find a way to totally cooperate with all other men, then God would be "dead" to him, for we would imagine that we no longer need Him.

Let us go down and confound their language . . .

THE ONLY UNITY THAT remains ever indivisible is the unity of the Godhead which is blessed forever. Thus, Father, Son and Holy Spirit came down to divide the dangerous unity of fallen man. The single most divisive factor is language. The Lord divided the nations by confounding the languages.

The judgment was an act of mercy, because total human unity is toxic when it is not based upon the only true center, the worship of the only true God and Jesus whom He has sent. God will not allow man to so empower himself that he utterly destroys all mankind. No longer would man be allowed to be "as one".

Paul would tell us centuries later that God divided the nations and even appointed their times and boundaries that, *"they might seek Him".*

Obviously it hasn't always worked out that the majority of nations did seek God, for free will is involved also. But the division of nations was a benevolent judgment, a safeguard against the humanly irresistible power of a globally united humanity with the capability to construct one unique "truth", equally acceptable and understood by all, with which to counter the Word of God.

So the building project came to an abrupt end, and the workers gathered into their own language groups and dispersed abroad to fill the earth. However, the dream of "making a name for ourselves" has never died out. One of the undercurrents of all subsequent human history has been the attempt to get back to a worldwide unity, to overcome the "Babel effect" and to complete the humanistic city and the tower.

The earth is littered with pyramids, ziggurats and astrological tower platforms, as a testimony to the universal truth of the story in Genesis 11. From Peru, to Mexico, to Egypt and Babylon, in China, Cambodia, indeed everywhere people have gathered, these artificial mountains have been built. The universality of the zodiac also testifies to the worldwide apostasy spoken of in Genesis.

The symbol of the unfinished tower is the inspiration for the European Union parliamentary building. The United Nations is also an attempt to bring about a world unity. We are approaching the time when, through technology, men will arrive at their closest attempt to overcome "the Babel effect" and come together "as one", in defiance of the very God who once divided us. This seems to be "their hour and the power of darkness". But according to Jesus and the prophets and apostles, it will be short lived.

The Modern Repudiation of Genesis 11

*The earth also is defiled under the inhabitants thereof; because **they have transgressed the laws, changed the ordinance, broken the everlasting covenant**. Therefore hath the curse devoured the earth, and they that dwell therein are desolate: therefore the inhabitants of the earth are burned, and few men left (Isaiah 24:5-6).*

GENESIS 1-11 CONTAINS A divine revelation of all that is basic to a true understanding of man; his world, his fall into sin and alienation from God, his present lost condition, and the possibility of his salvation.

It contains truths that are universal, in that they apply to all men, and not just to the church or to Israel. All men are created in the image of God, (though we have shattered and distorted that image). All men share in the sin of Adam, and have original sin. Marriage is for all people, male and female.

Genesis 1-11 is truth. In other words, it is reality. The human race truly did all descend *"from one blood"* as Paul told us in Acts 17. There are truly God-given roles for male and female to live out, and marriage is an objective reality, not a mere social construct. There really was a worldwide Flood, which altered the geography, lifespan, and the weather patterns of the earth.

A civilization which has been largely based upon the acceptance and recognition of these primal truths cannot help but flourish for it is based upon reality. The extent to which any human enterprise is based upon reality, i.e., "true truth" as Francis Schaeffer used to call it, is the extent to which it will prosper.

The Judeo-Christian West has flourished for centuries, expanding and developing into the greatest, most powerful, secure, prosperous beneficial civilization which have ever existed. The West's liberal, democratic republics have afforded to the most people, the greatest freedoms ever known to any on earth.

But now the West is dying.

The second psalm is a prophecy, which explains it all so well.

> Why do the heathen rage, and the people imagine a vain thing? The kings of the earth set themselves, and the rulers take counsel together, against the Lord, and against his anointed, saying, Let us break their bands asunder, and cast away their cords from us (Psalm 2).

The expression, *"kings of the earth and the rulers"*, should not be understood to refer only to our government officials. The phrase refers rather to all of the leaders in education, government, religion, academia, the intellectuals, news and media, the opinion shapers and molders, and entertainers, who have achieved among themselves a remarkable consensus.

Our ruling elites, the so called *"kings of the earth and the rulers"*, have for too long *"taken counsel together against the Lord and His Christ"*. Where have they taken this godless counsel? In my view, they have been taken it for the past eighty years or so to the institutions of higher learning.

It is for many of us an all too familiar story. You scrimp and sacrifice to send a son or daughter to the university. They come home after the first semester saturated with "environmental awareness". By the end of the first year they have adapted progressive notions about economics, taxes and "social justice". Eventually they are holding to feminist positions and hate America. After about four years, if the brainwashing does its work, they are virulently anti-Israel,

The psalmist predicted that the ruling class elite, would launch a misguided liberation movement against the very foundations that undergird our blessed and once prosperous societies. They preach, *"Let us break their bands asunder ... let us cast aside their cords."*

Whose bands? The Lord and His Anointed (Christ)! Whose cords? Has the Lord and His Messiah put us in bondage? Are their societal cords that have been cut and cast aside?

I believe that one of the evils of our day and the reason for our rapid societal decline has been this very thing. Our elites are in rebellion against reality! They are leading a "liberation movement" against Judeo-Christian moral teaching, seeking to throw it all out!

They are repudiating, everything that Genesis 1-11 says about reality, point by point.

Consider the contrasts

Genesis 1-11	Modern revolutionary ethos
Worship Creator	Worship the creation
God Created everything	Impersonal time & chance; evolution
Man made in God's image	Man as highly evolved animal
Man as steward of the earth	Man as blight/disease on earth
Marriage; male and female	Sexual anarchy; decide for yourselves
Two distinct gender roles	Gender as a mere construct

"Be fruitful and multiply"........ZPG; Children as an unwanted burden
Every seed bearing fruit..............................Genetically modified "seed"
Death penalty for murder.............No death penalty (except abortion)
Man to spread out & subdue the earth ....
....Earth to be protected from man's destruction
Nations of the world to be separated..................... The United Nations
You are allowed to eat meat...Vegetarianism

I could go on and on. It seems like man has repudiated everything that God ordained for man in Genesis 1-11.

Our atheistic leadership elites are trying to remake the world in their own image, which is a godless utopia. But this puts us all on a collision course with the God of the Bible, who has His own purpose for this world.

Christ or Cain?

*For this is the message that ye heard from the beginning, that we should love one another. **Not as Cain, who was of that wicked one,** and slew his brother. And wherefore slew he him? Because his own works were evil, and his brother's righteous. Marvel not, my brethren, if the world hate you. We know that we have passed from death unto life, because we love the brethren. He that loveth not his brother abideth in death. Whosoever hateth his brother is a murderer: and ye know that no murderer hath eternal life abiding in him (1 John 3:11-15).*

THERE ARE ONLY TWO types of people, God lovers or God haters. This is the teaching of the Bible all the way through to the end. This concept is found in the Ten Commandments, notably in the second commandment of God,

> Thou shalt not make unto thee any graven image, or any likeness of any thing that is in heaven above, or that is in the earth beneath, or that is in the water under the earth. Thou shalt not bow down thyself to them, nor serve them: for I the LORD thy God am a jealous God, visiting the iniquity of the fathers upon the children unto the third and fourth generation of **them that hate me**; And shewing

> mercy unto thousands of them that love me, and
> keep my commandments (Exodus 20).

There is no third category of humanity. There are and can only be either God haters, or God lovers. Neutrality is impossible, for indifference to God is the acme of ungodliness. It is pride and hatred according to the Word of God.

There are consequently only two spiritualities. People either worship God via the way made through the God-ordained sacrifice, or they end up will worshipping, on their own terms and making their own sacrifice.

The first way leads to love, which is born in the heart of the worshipper as a consequence of the mercy of the God who ordained a sacrifice, and who would Himself become the sacrifice. Love is the fruit of eternal life. The love of God, for God and man is born in the heart of the believer.

The second way, demands a sacrifice also, but never leads to love, for it is not based on humble gratitude, but on willful self-justification.

The apostle John brings this out in his First Epistle. To the Lord's apostle there are only two paradigms for all of humanity: Christ or Cain.

Love one another is what we have been hearing from the start, i.e., at the onset of our Christian walk. Love pervades the Gospels, the Epistles, the story of Jesus. Indeed, it permeates the whole concept of God seeing us in our sin and misery and sending His Son to suffer in our place as a substitute. Love permeates Christian spirituality.

Yes, love is commanded. But even if it were not, it is so implied that since we have been so loved, in such an unworthy state, how could we not gratefully love one another? The paradigm for those who have truly received the gift of life is Jesus, whose love for God and for us was acted out in the Incarnation, and on the cross in the giving up of His own life, and in our subsequent adoption into His family.

But John suggests a second paradigm, one which he warns us not to emulate, for it is the sure sign of spiritual death and darkness; that is Cain. We are told that Cain was "of the wicked one". That is, he lived out his life at the disposal of and in the character of the devil.

Cain "slew his brother". The word "slew" here has a religious and sacramental significance. In other words there is a sense in which Cain offered up his brother as a sacrifice, just as Abel offered up a lamb as a sacrifice. Abel "slew a lamb"; Cain "slew his brother".

The whole story of Cain and Abel centers around sacrifice, remember? Both brothers worshipped, both acknowledged God, and both "drew near" with gifts. But God openly accepted Abel's offering, and openly rejected Cain's. What was the difference between these two offerings and why was one accepted and the other rejected?

Offerings to God are theological statements. When Abel came before the God-appointed altar, with the broken body of a bleeding lamb of the flock in his hands, he was making a statement. "Dear Creator, I have sinned against You and deserve to die for it under Your judgment. But You have appointed a substitute to die in my place and this lamb is a token of that substitute. Receive me in the name of the substitute You have appointed."

This is the theology of the first martyr, substitutionary death, the presupposition of sin and wrath, the necessity for a sacrifice for sin, the humble dependence on the God-appointed sacrifice for forgiveness and acceptance, and the patient endurance of persecution for the truth.

But what was the theology of the first murderer? Cain was willing to acknowledge God as his Creator, thus he offered the fruit of the ground which God had blessed. But he refused the bloody substitute offering, and rejected the presuppositions that underlie it, i.e., the wrath of God, guilt, death as a penalty for sin, and judgment for sin, which is satisfied only in the God-appointed sacrifice. Unlike Abel, he saw no need for redemption.

But notice that though perhaps he felt he was above slaying a lamb to offer to God, he didn't hesitate to slay his brother. In other words, sacrifice is inevitable. Someone is going to have to pay for sin. Someone is going to be offered up on an altar to a god, if not the true sacrifice to the only true God.

Cain offered Abel up to his own rage, on the altar of his hurt feelings, envy, and rebellion. Thus Cain "slew" his brother. He wouldn't kill a lamb but he killed his brother. He wouldn't offer to God, but he offered to himself! But in all religion, true or false, sacrifice is going to be offered no matter what!

Why did he slay his brother? Because his own works were evil, and his brother's were righteous.

Cain actually hated his brother for doing right, for coming to God in the God-appointed way! It was because his brother's righteousness showed up his own faux righteousness that Cain killed Abel. He "slew" him for being good, and because he himself was determined to remain a sinner!

It was because we are sinners and Jesus is good, (sinless) that Jesus was slain and offered to God for us.

> And he made his grave with the wicked, and with the rich in his death; because he had done no violence, neither was any deceit in his mouth. Yet it pleased the LORD to bruise him; he hath put him to grief: **when thou shalt make his soul an offering for sin**, he shall see his seed, he shall prolong his days, and the pleasure of the LORD shall prosper in his hand (Isaiah 53:9-10).

All people worship someone or something, and of course

all worship requires sacrifice. There is no question of it, it is inevitable. The only question is, will it be the God-appointed sacrifice, or the humanistic, self-serving sacrifice? Humanity is incurably religious in spite of the best efforts of atheists.

Humanists in our nation have disavowed God, the Bible, worship, prayer, and spirituality. They believe the message of the cross is degrading to man's dignity, with its underlying presupposition of the wrath of God, divine justice, and the sacrifice of Jesus as a substitute. How degrading to man! Man has "evolved" past such primitive and barbaric religion!

But these same secularists have just passed the milestone of the fifty millionth "legal" abortion in the United States alone! Abortion is definitely a sacrifice to a false god.

There are only two paradigms for humanity.

The first model is Christ, who offered Himself as a sacrifice for our sins, to avert the wrath of a just and holy God against sin and sinners. He laid down His life for us! He poured out His life as an offering! He took nothing from us, rather He gave us His life.

The other model is Cain, who is above and beyond all of that, too "humane" to kill a lamb, too proud to concede guilt and the danger of wrath. Cain wouldn't worship God as anything more than his Creator. He felt he needed no redeemer substitute.

But someone had to pay, therefore Cain "slew His brother". He offered his brother's life as an offering to his own rage, jealousy, and insecurity. In little and big ways the world is full of Cains, making others pay by killing them.

> And he said, What hast thou done? the voice of thy brother's blood crieth unto me from the ground. And now art thou cursed from the earth, which hath opened her mouth to receive thy broth-

er's blood from thy hand; When thou tillest the ground, it shall not henceforth yield unto thee her strength; a fugitive and a vagabond shalt thou be in the earth. And Cain said unto the Lord, My punishment is greater than I can bear. Behold, thou hast driven me out this day from the face of the earth; and from thy face shall I be hid; and I shall be a fugitive and a vagabond in the earth; and it shall come to pass, that every one that findeth me shall slay me. And the Lord said unto him, Therefore whosoever slayeth Cain, vengeance shall be taken on him sevenfold. And the Lord set a mark upon Cain, lest any finding him should kill him (Genesis 4:10-15).

Endnotes

1   John C. Whitcomb, *The Early Earth*, Baker Books, Grand Rapids, MI, 1972, p. 111

2   Edward Wharton, *Redemption is Planned, Needed, Provided*, Howard Books, 1972. I am indebted for this quote to an Apologeticspress.org tract entitled *Genesis 1-11; Myth or History?*

3   Edward J. Young, *Studies in Genesis One*, Baker Books, Grand Rapids, MI, 1975

4   Henry Morris, *The Genesis Record*, Baker Books, Grand Rapids, MI, 2009, p. 23

5   Henry Morris, *The Genesis Record*

6   (http://www.dailymail.co.uk/sciencetech/article-1203405/Guardian-planets-Jupiter-Saturn-shield-Earth-catastrophic-comet-collisions.html), accessed 12/22/2015

7   Henry Morris, *The Genesis Record*, pg 80-81

8   G. H. Pember, *Earth's Earliest Ages*, Kregel Academic & Professional; Reprint edition, 1975

9   Was it at the place of the cherubim with the flaming sword? Perhaps it was, for in the time of the tabernacle of Moses, God appointed figures of cherubim to be woven into the curtain of the Holy Place where priests drew near to God in the temple.

10 I personally believe that fire fell on it and consumed it, but admittedly that is speculation. We don't know, because Scripture only tells us that God did accept it in a visible way.

ing a ags fine5?? f???????

11 Erich Sauer, *Dawn of World Redemption*, Paternoster Press; New edition edition, 1985, p. 64

12 It is believed that the Greek god "Vulcan", the god of fire and smithing, was from a corrupted memory of Tubal Cain . . . "Bal-Cain" . . . Vulcan.

13 Jesus would tell us centuries later that "The children of this age, are often much wiser in their time, than the children of light" (Luke 16:8).

14 G. H. Pember, *Earth's Earliest Ages*. Note: By no means do I endorse everything Pember taught, but he did have some valuable insights.

15 Ibid.

16 Ibid.

17 I want you to know that I have not seen this movie nor would I ever encourage anyone to see it. Such things are damning and corrupting to the soul. I read a synopsis of the movie and was stunned that there were at the same time, several other similar offerings.

18 A. W. Pink, *Gleanings in Genesis*, Watchmaker Publishing, 2011

19 Henry Morris, *The Genesis Record*

20 Alford Eidersheim, *Life and Times Of Jesus the Messiah*, Hendrickson Publishing

21 Erich Sauer, *Dawn of World Redemption*

22 I am heavily indebted to Dr Henry Morris's *Genesis Record* for this section.

23 Henry Morris, *God and the Nations*, Master Books, 2003

Other Books
by Pastor Bill Randles

Making War in the Heavenlies: A different look at Spiritual Warfare- (1994) Pastor Bill was asked in 1994 to explain why he wasn't leading his church into various aspects of city wide spiritual warfare exercising, such as prayer walking, March for Jesus, naming the demons over the city, binding and loosing ,etc. Out of that explanation came this book, which discusses not only the heretical practices listed above, bit the true biblical teaching on spiritual warfare.

Weighed and Found Wanting: Putting the Toronto Blessing in Context- (1995)- Thousands of Christians were traveling to the Toronto Airport Vineyard to experience "a new anointing", and Spiritual Drunkeness. Was this really "as a rushing mighty wind from heaven" as its proponents claimed? Pastor Bill refutes this notion, having traced the "revival" back to its roots in the Manifested Sons of God heresy, once rebuked and rejected by the Assemblies of God, but now widely accepted as a mighty revival.

Born From Above: An Exposition of John Chapter 3 (2015) - This is an exposition of the third chapter of the Gospel of John, one of the most familiar and beloved chapters in the New Testament. In this brief study,Pastor Bill shows the continuity of the theme, the New Birth as taught by Jesus, in a conversation with one of the greatest and most renown theologians of his day, Nicodemus. Pastor Bill Sheds new light on familiar texts such as John 3:16. This book is expositional and evangelistic as well. It would be great for Bible Studies.

Mending The Nets: Themes and Commentary of First John - In this book Pastor Bill explores the undergirding themes of first John, such as eternal life, the tests of eternal life, true and false faith, the Gnostic redefinition of the knowledge of God, and the true knowledge of God. Like John, Pastor Bill takes us back to the beginning, the first thing revealed in the gospel of Jesus . This commentary is relevant to the current apostasy in the church.

A Sword On The Land: The Muslim World in Bible Prophecy - (2013) The 2011 "Arab Spring" was significant, but not for the reasons the world hoped for. Pastor Bill, in a very readable style, explains that rather than being a movement towards democracy in the Arab world, the real significance was the setting in place of the nations of the Middle East for the fulfillment of endgames prophecies.

34401514R00135

Made in the USA
San Bernardino, CA
27 May 2016